SOUL BELIEFS

SOUL BELIEFS

REMOVING THE OBSTACLES THAT PREVENT BREAKTHROUGH AND INTIMACY WITH GOD

TAMMY J. HERNANDEZ

ISBN: 978-1-953314-04-8

Library of Congress Control Number: 2020916056

Published by:

Messenger Books
1629 Brookhollow, Dr.
Lindale, TX 75771

messenger
BOOKS

Messengerbooks.com

This book is dedicated to the Lover of my soul.

I am Yours and You are mine!

CONTENTS

PART I

GOING BEHIND CLOSED DOORS

1

THIS CAN'T BE HAPPENING

I stood next to him, the man who I had feared all my life. Things had been going as well as could be expected. Then, out of nowhere, as if it could no longer hide itself, it sprang into action. The violence and anger that I had known so well growing up, was once again glaring back at me.

This wasn't the way it was supposed to be. When I found out that he was dying of lung cancer, I had prayed. The visit was supposed to include healing, forgiveness, and restoration. I had prayed that the violent man that I had called my dad would somehow be different now that he was facing the end of his life.

I had no desire to see him break or grovel in regret. All I wanted was to hear the words, "I love you." I already had my forgiveness wrapped up like a gift, ready to give to him. Truthfully, I had forgiven him many years before. I was so anxious to tell him, once again, that there was a loving God that understood him and had His arms wide open, offering him forgiveness.

I had dreamed that I would crawl into his hospital bed and finally be held by a "Daddy." I longed for his acceptance and approval because he had made it very clear to me, for as long as I could remember, that I just wasn't enough. I really thought that he would have taken that final opportunity to tell me he loved me, but those weren't the words coming out of his mouth.

As he screamed at me to get the f___ out, I stood frozen, out of shock, but mostly out of fear. This man had put my mom in the hospital too many times for me to count. He had slammed my youngest brother against the wall, holding him up by the throat. I had seen, on countless occasions, what he was capable of. As I stood within inches of his clenched fists, it didn't matter that I was 45 years old; I instantly became that terrified little girl, the one that I had been running from my entire life.

Soul Beliefs & Scar Tissue

My intent in pulling back the curtain of my life is not to glorify the violence or speak derogatory of anyone. Instead, it's to reveal how the enemy of our soul tries to engrave his lies onto our hearts through rejection, disappointment, abuse, and more.

Regardless of your childhood, each of us has and will experience pain in this world. Whether it is through hurtful words, abuse, or betrayal, it is the goal of the enemy to create invisible, internal scars that he wants to use to negatively influence us. He wants our souls to come to conclusions that are contradictory to what God says. I call these negative soul beliefs.

Like internal adhesions in your body that are not easily discovered by CT scans, MRI's, or x-rays, soul beliefs can restrict or limit our freedom without us even realizing they exist. It is possible to live with these unidentified beliefs, even if you've been through deliverance, inner healing, or counseling; all of which, I am a big proponent. I believe it takes the unveiling of the Holy Spirit to uncover what our soul really believes.

I know from first-hand experience that it is possible to be a committed, Bible believing, lover of God and still have these undetected beliefs in your soul. While we all "scar" in varying degrees, depending on what we've already experienced, none of us are exempt from the bumps and bruises of life. So, it is important for us to:

1) Be able to identify a soul belief
2) Know what to do with them
3) Learn how to prevent the negative ones
4) Allow the Holy Spirit to write new, positive soul beliefs

Soul beliefs can manifest themselves in many ways. They can cause us to turn to works and legalism. They often cause us to reject ourselves and others. They rob us of intimacy, bind us with fear, and so much more. Regardless of the many ways in which they affect us, the end result is bondage in one degree or another.

As we move through these chapters, we will talk about some common soul beliefs and how they manifest in things like shame, fear, rejection, and more. Once we've identified them, we'll learn how to deal with and be healed from these hidden scars. And lastly, we'll expose how soul beliefs are formed, so you can prevent them. As I take you on this journey, it is my prayer that you will encounter the Father in all His love and glory.

A Painful Start

My earliest memories are of fear. From as far back as I can remember, I worried that I, or someone else, would do something to light my dad's short fuse. I knew it didn't take much, so I lived in a constant state of hyper-awareness. I lived with a few unspoken directives: keep everything under control, be as good as possible, and don't upset anyone. As early as five I can remember feeling like it was my job to control everything and everyone around me just to keep my dad from "losing it." No one ever told me that it was my responsibility. No one needed to. It was just an automatic response to the conditions in which I lived. Like Pavlov's dogs, I had unknowingly been trained, because at the ring of a bell, he would explode.

Christmases were always the worst. I don't know if it was the financial pressure or the demons of my dad's past, but the holidays were explosive. Despite my best efforts not to, the little girl in me would long for Christmas to be a happy occasion, only to find myself disappointed again. Without realizing it, I developed a love/hate relationship with hope and unknowingly concluded that hope wasn't a very good friend. Disappointment and sadness seemed more reliable. As a little girl trapped in this situation, I did my very best to stifle hope because the *disappointment* was even more painful than the crisis itself.

I wish I could tell you that the anger only came out near the holidays, but that would be a lie. The truth is, I don't remember there being very many good days. That might be because they were so far and few in between, or it could be that the violence had more power to imprint itself in my memory

Either way, I could be in my room playing "school" with my sister and the rising level of noise would send an emergency-alert that we were headed for an event. As a six-year-old, there wasn't much I could do to stop it, but I would try. If I saw a fight starting with words, I'd try to distract my mom. I remember wondering, "Can't she see the signs?"

The thing that made it difficult was that even if he seemed like he was in a good mood, which was rare and usually at the beginning of his drinking, it would change at the blink of an eye. There was no real "pattern" to help us detect it. The only reliable thing about it was that it happened quickly and regularly.

On one occasion, my parents were already entrenched in the throes of a fight. My sister was trying to get us, the kids, out of the front door. Although I couldn't see my mom, I did get a glimpse of my dad. His hands were dripping with blood. As we stood on the front lawn, screaming and crying, my dad walked by and threatened us, "If you don't stop crying, I'm gonna…" When the paramedics brought my mom out to the ambulance, I honestly didn't know if she was dead or alive. For many years, I had the same dream over and over about my dad killing all of us.

At one point, my mom tried to get away from my father by taking us, her four children, from Florida to Indiana. I remember feeling relieved and yet terribly sad at the same time because I missed him. I loved him. I still wanted a daddy. So, when they got back together, it was a double-edged sword. I wanted to believe that the "reconciliation" had changed them and that we would live happily ever after, but the fighting didn't stop.

When you grow up like that, it changes you from within. Those formative years are supposed to be when safety, protection, unconditional love, and acceptance are all building the "you," or "the foundation" on which the "you" will be built. Each member of my family experienced different things with my dad. We were all scarred in various ways, and our different personalities caused each of us to receive and process it differently. Nonetheless, my father embedded a deep handprint on each of us.

As If Things Weren't Bad Enough

The next chapter of our lives wasn't much better. My mom and dad divorced when I was about six or seven. One day, he just seemed to disappear. For nearly a year, I didn't know if he was dead or alive.

My mom remarried, and I'd like to tell you that he was a good stepfather, but he wasn't. He too was abusive. There was no such thing as spankings, but there were beatings. He would start with one object and, if it broke, move on to another. Once again, we never knew what it was going to be that would set him off, only that it happened frequently. Sometimes just the sight of one of the kids would send him into a tailspin. The other problem was that he was a child molester. Things were certainly worse.

We hadn't seen or heard from our dad for more than a year when we received a message from a family friend that he was trying to reach us. We knew not to tell our mom or stepfather because he had reiterated, on numerous occasions, that if he ever saw our father, he would kill him. So we met with him in secret. My dad informed us that he had been hospitalized for a nervous breakdown. (I later found out that he had to have numerous shock treatments.) He told us that he was better and wanted to be a part of our lives. Once he knew what was going on with our stepfather, he gave us the option to come live with him. I can't tell you for sure what was going on in my eight-year-old little heart. I wanted to be with my mom, but I had to get away from my stepfather. No child should ever have to make that kind of decision.

Despite all the horrible things my dad had done, I wanted to believe that he had changed. After all, I had literally been dreaming of the day he would come and rescue us. In my mind and dreams, he would always return a hero, as a daddy should be. So, when we were given a choice, my sister and I painfully decided to go with our father, while my two brothers chose to stay with our mom. At such a young age, I had to look at my mom and tell her that I no longer wanted to live with her. There is no way that I can make you understand how painful that was. It felt like I was literally ripping my mom's heart right out of her chest. Just a couple years later, my stepfather did the most horrific thing of all, he set my youngest brother on fire. By the grace of God, and after many months in the hospital with major skin grafts, my little brother survived.

A Chance to Start Over

For the next several years, my sister and I bounced around from Florida to Indiana with our father. There were times that I didn't even know who I lived near. One time my father forgot to pick me up from school, and I couldn't recall one single family member or friend that I could call for help. After sitting alone at the school in the dark for hours, I finally remembered the name of the bar that he frequented. Sure enough, he was there.

I will admit, he seemed different at first. I found it easy to forgive him because I loved him and just wanted things to be better. I think in any abusive or neglectful relationship, the "desire for things to be okay" is **so** great that the victim will tolerate all kinds of things, all the while, holding out hope that things will change. While my father had "improved" as far as not being physically abusive, at least to my sister and I, life was still filled with neglect, anger, and severe poverty.

Our living arrangements were not always ideal. For a while, we lived in a "house" that had no bathroom. We literally had an "outhouse." And, since we didn't have a bathroom, that meant going to school with greasy hair and filthy old clothes. Yep, the kids had a hay-day with me. It was rather common to have our utilities turned off, and while living in the northern state of Indiana, we had to count pennies to scrounge up enough money to get fuel to heat up our little garage apartment. This was my "normal." It was all I knew, so I just learned to make the best of it.

For several years, it was just my sister and I that lived with our dad. Off and on through the years, my brothers would come to visit and sometimes live with us for short periods of time. I remember on one occasion, all four of us were fighting over a single can of corn because that was all we had to eat in the apartment.

Still, I just assumed that my dad was doing the best he could. I just knew he had to love us, so this had to be beyond his control. It never occurred to me, as a child, that if he weren't drinking all his money away, he could have taken better care of us.

When I was about ten-years-old, my sister and father had a falling out, and she went to live with our mom. For several years, it was just my dad and I. Sadly, he put me in so many risky situations. I remember being left in the front seat of my dad's old pickup truck, in the middle of an Indiana winter, while my dad sat inside the bar, drinking for hours into the night. I don't know which was worse, not being able to get warm or the fear of being outside in the dark parking lot by myself. I think I was about ten years old.

My dad and I eventually moved into a "real" house! It was on an 18-acre "tropical hammock" in Vero Beach, Fl. I know, it sounds beautiful, right? So, what's the problem? Well, it was in the famous, but by then, abandoned McKee Jungle Gardens, one of Florida's earliest tourist attractions. It had been abandoned for about five years, and it had the maggots to prove it. If that wasn't bad enough, the guy that was letting us stay there was a complete drunkard. I can honestly say that I never once saw him sober. That was a good thing, though! Because he always drank to oblivion, he was easier to fight off when he would try to "mess" with me.

Even though my dad had not laid an abusive hand on me for a while, I knew better than to make him upset. I did everything I could to avoid making him angry. I lived in a constant state of performance and fear. As hard as I tried, I just wasn't perfect. If I forgot to lay out meat for dinner before leaving for school, that meant I wouldn't have dinner ready for him when he got home from a long, hard day at work. Of course, most ten-year-old kids aren't thinking about that as they head off to school, so I forgot on a few occasions. Unfortunately, there were even days that I didn't have the house cleaned in time. I just couldn't successfully juggle school, cooking, and cleaning as well as I wanted to, and that didn't go over well with my father.

My dad was big, and I had seen him in action, so when he got mad, I was terrified! I promised that I would do better, and I tried even harder to please him. I blamed myself because, after all, it's not that hard to remember to lay something out for dinner. I knew I could do better, and I vowed to do so. He didn't need to physically punish me any longer; his anger and disapproval were enough.

Having fun or enjoying friends was out of the question. There was no way that I was going to bring anyone to my house. Instead, most of my Saturdays or Sundays were filled with cleaning, cooking, and laundry. Since we didn't have a washing machine or dryer, my dad would take me to the laundromat every couple of weeks and drop me off. He would come back several hours later. I remember once counting how many loads I had to do, and to this day, I remember the record was twenty loads.

With everything I experienced, I would say the most difficult part was dealing with all the women he would bring home. Sadly, they didn't bother to protect me from what was happening. I was exposed to things that no child should ever see or hear. Thankfully, I knew how to deal with it: I'd simply stuff it. Whatever it took to keep my dad from being mad at me, I'd do.

When my younger brother came to live with us, he wasn't as "trained" on the way things were done at our dad's house. He was a very active and adorable little guy. And, even though I had successfully been able to escape my father's abuse since returning, I can't say the same was true for my little brother. My father was so cruel to him. I'll just leave it at that.

I'd Had Enough

I lived like that until I was about to enter Junior High. We moved more times than I can literally recall. I was living in the abandoned McKee Jungle Gardens at the time that I decided I'd had enough!

My father's girlfriend at the time, a "newly retired" prostitute, was now pregnant with, what they thought, was my father's child. The violence between them was more than I could handle. Also, the years of being humiliated by my dad in front of his drunk friends had taken a toll on me. I had reached my limit. If there was any chance of a different life, I wanted it.

I was in my early teens, and I had no respectable female influence, so when I found out that my mom was divorcing my first stepfather, I decided to move in with her. Once again, I found myself in the position of having to break one of my parent's hearts. It was not easy to leave my dad. I felt like I was responsible for him. I wondered who would cook and clean for him. The truth is, with all his faults, I still loved him deeply.

Somehow, I managed to make the move. My emotions were all over the place. I was excited about the possibility of having a "normal" life, but I still felt like I had betrayed my dad, just as I had done to my mom years before.

So, I set off for a new life with my mom. We moved to Gainesville, which was about five hours from my dad. It wasn't a smooth transition, though. The years of hearing my dad talk so badly about my mom had influenced me. Besides, my mom and I didn't really *know* one another because I had really grown up with my dad. Sure, I had seen her off and on through the years, but we didn't really *know* one another. And, sadly for her, she got me just as those lovely teenage years were in full bloom.

For the first time in my life, I didn't have someone that I *feared* in authority over me. Unfortunately, I had no respect for my mom, and I showed it. I was so full of anger. My mom wasn't doing very well, either. She had been through the wringer with both my dad and her second husband. All her dreams of having a wonderful family had long since been destroyed. She made decisions that I know she regrets, and I treated her in ways that I regret.

When I was about sixteen, my mom remarried. All I knew was that no man was going to tell me what to do again! That attitude didn't go over very well, and I was kicked out at seventeen, during my senior year of high school.

As challenging as the next two years would end up being, they served an unknown purpose. They were unknowingly moving me closer to the moment that would forever change me.

2

WHEN EVERYTHING CHANGED

AN ENCOUNTER WITH JESUS

*I*t was 1986, and I was just 19 years old. It had been two years since I had been kicked out. I had graduated from high school with a couple small scholarships. During those two years, I lived in everything from the top of a pickup truck camper in the back of someone's yard to finally sharing a house with a few people. I was working at a medical clinic and putting myself through the local community college. Even with all my "outward progress," I was still broken inside, making choices that I wish I hadn't.

I had an awareness of God. I believed that He existed. I even prayed. However, there was no evidence of God being involved in my life. To me, He was sort of like a far off "wishing star" or the hope of something better when I died. The weird thing, though, was that I found myself wanting to please this invisible God.

There was a woman that I worked with at the clinic. She was kind and friendly. I never felt judged by her, even though she knew some of what I was doing. We were talking one day, and I asked her straight up whether what I was doing was "sin" and if I'd go to hell. I can't explain it, but somehow, she was able to tell me the truth in such a loving way that I never got the impression that God was disgusted or angry with me.

She invited me to church, and I accepted. I had been to church when I was little. Our neighbors were Christians, and they had asked us several times to come to their church. They knew what was going on in our home. They had seen the police at our house, my mom rushed to the hospital, and four little kids screaming in the front yard way too many times.

As a kid, I loved going to my neighbor's church. I would get up early on most Sundays, hair in pigtails, and wait outside for the bus to pick me up for Sunday School. Sometime around the age of six, during a special children's program, I prayed the "sinner's prayer" and asked Jesus to come into my heart. I even got baptized.

Since I had not been to church after the time I was a little girl, I found myself excited about the upcoming visit. I met her there that Sunday. It was a lovely service, and I immediately made plans to return the following week. However, during the week, I had many questions rolling through my mind. There were some things in my life that I was pretty sure God might have a problem with. At the same time, there were some things in my life that IF God did have a problem with them, then I would have had a problem with Him. As I wrestled with these thoughts all week, I anxiously waited for Sunday.

Sunday finally came, and as I sat and listened to the preacher, I was utterly shocked that he was talking about the very things that I had been wrestling with all week long! It was as if God Himself had told the pastor to speak directly to me. In thirty-plus years since, I have never heard another preacher talk about the same topics. God spoke through that man to let me know what He thought about those "deal-breaker" topics. I couldn't believe my ears.

I don't recall the pastor inviting anyone forward for prayer. As a matter of fact, I don't remember much of anything except finding myself at the altar weeping uncontrollably. I had an encounter with Jesus. A beautiful collision had occurred that would forever change me.

It Was Easy to Love Jesus

Although I wasn't completely different overnight, things really started changing in and for me. A couple of months before giving my life to Jesus, I had broken up with the guy I had been dating since high school. We were just two weeks away from getting married when I found out that he was cheating on me.

After the broken engagement, I had a good amount of time to get to know this "new Man" in my life. I really didn't know much about God or about being a Christian, so I began to devour the Bible, and it was as if the world came alive.

Although I was still hurting from the broken relationship and the trouble of my past, I began to feel life stirring inside of me. It was a fight to get past the pain and rejection, but it was in there. It sort of felt like I was on life support and God's Word was the IV that was giving me life-sustaining fluid. It seemed as if I was Jesus' only patient and I had all His attention. I was experiencing a relationship with Him that I had never imagined was possible.

The next several years were like the most fabulous honeymoon. Looking back, I can now see that my life changed dramatically, even though it didn't seem that way at the time. It was so easy to accept and fall in love with Jesus. He made me feel so loved. He was healing my wounds, and I was growing stronger.

After about six or seven months, I moved to another city and found a great church. About a year and a half later, my ex-fiancé contacted me and tried to get back together. I couldn't believe it. I had been praying for that very thing to happen because I still thought I loved him. I wanted him to meet Jesus, too, so we could get married and live "happily ever after." By the time he tried to get back together, my life had changed so much. I just knew he wasn't the one for me. I was convinced that God had someone better for me, a man of God.

As I waited for that to happen, God brought me some amazing friends. I had a church that genuinely felt more like a family. I began to experience a kind of acceptance that I had never known. At first, I didn't want people to know about my past. They knew the "new" Tammy, and that was all I wanted them to know. As time went on, I slowly let people know *some* of my past. To my surprise, they loved me anyway. That continued to fuel the hope that I could have the kind of life that I had dreamed of and, more importantly, the type of marriage that I had always hoped was possible.

I still had plenty in my life that needed to be healed. I think Jesus worked on the most urgent things at first. If a patient is brought into the emergency room with multiple injuries from a car wreck, the doctors and nurses are going to work on the most life-threatening injuries first. As those are taken care of, their attention can then turn to less critical injuries. God knew just how to nurse me back to life.

I felt like an ugly caterpillar wrapped in a cocoon. Instead of being in that dark place alone, Jesus was in there with me. And since I longed to be a beautiful butterfly, I continued to let Him work in me.

One of my favorite songs when I first gave my heart to Jesus was by Roby Duke, called "Carpenter."[1] I would go to the beach or inter-coastal waterway and sit in my car and blast that song as loudly as I could and cry my eyes out. It best represented my life and how I felt. I soaked in the heart-melting words of complete surrender, crying out for restoration of all the broken pieces of my own heart and life.

Those years were painful yet glorious. They were filled with so many miracles. From bouts of depression to moments of sheer happiness, I experienced Jesus' faithfulness. I honestly felt that I was the love of **His** life. You couldn't have convinced me that I wasn't His favorite, until…

Dream Come True?

After what seemed like *forever*, God miraculously brought into my life a wonderful man of God. It wasn't always easy waiting for that to happen, but I had been determined to wait on God. I desperately wanted Him involved in the process. I felt like God told me that I wouldn't need to date around to find the "right one," but that He would "bring us together." I'm not saying everyone should take this approach, but it was what I wanted and honestly believed that God had told me.

I won't go into it all, but let me just say, God did not let me down! Our story is miraculous. When Roger asked me to marry him, I knew beyond a shadow of a doubt that God was in it. I was confident that I was going to continue this incredible adventure with Jesus but now with someone to love right by my side.

Everything I had hoped and believed for was happening right before my eyes. I had the assurance and the confirmations that this scared, young woman needed. I just knew that since we were doing it "God's way" that it was going to be AMAZING! And, it was…for all of a day, well, not even a day.

No Longer Just Me and Jesus

I'll admit it, Roger had big shoes to fill. It had been just "Jesus-n-Tammy sitting in a tree" for so long. As I mentioned before, it had been like one long, incredible honeymoon with God. I had been loved by Jesus Himself.

I'll also admit, my expectations were off the charts. The dreams that I had of us being the *perfect*, "godly" married couple quickly disappeared. After seeing what my parents had gone through, I just *assumed* that when two Christians got married, especially when it was in such a "miraculous" way, that it would be great, at least most of the time. Or, if not most of the time, would it be great some of the time?

We had prepared by going to pre-marital counseling and even marriage conferences **before** we said, "I do." We read books on marriage. We listened to marriage tapes. We had pastoral input and support. We were "so" prepared. At least, we thought we were!

Our first big fight was the day after our wedding. I've since heard many people say that they fought on their honeymoon, too. I guess it isn't as "unusual" as I once thought. If this happened to you, I hope it was minor and quickly resolved. However, for us, it was a complicated issue, and we had no idea what to do about it.

The Greatest Disappointment

It would take a book dedicated to marriage alone to explain all that we went through in our first eight years together. It was the most painful of all my experiences in life, even my abusive childhood. I think the reason it was so much more difficult was that I had finally let my hopes fly high. I had put my trust in God and His promises about love and marriage, only to be disappointed again! The one Person (God) that I thought would *never* let me down, now appeared to be like all the others who couldn't be trusted.

It didn't take long for it to go from terrible to worse. The disappointment that we both experienced took our feet out from beneath us. It was a crushing blow. Every time we thought it couldn't get worse, it did. We prayed, prayed and prayed some more. We went to counseling. We attended more marriage conferences. We honestly did everything we could think of, but it only got worse.

No one seemed to know how to help us, either. On the outside, we were doing everything that we had been taught. I remember pastors and counselors being thoroughly stumped, unable to offer us any more advice. So, we would move on to another pastor or counselor. The more we tried, the more disappointed we became.

We could not figure out why "God was not helping us." This triggered abandonment issues in me. The six years before getting married had been remarkable. I had felt loved and accepted as I had never experienced in my life. Then, overnight, after saying, "I do," Jesus seemed to disappear. I know it sounds crazy, but it truly felt like Jesus went out and found this man so he could drop me off and split! I thought He must have realized who I *"really"* was, and **He didn't approve of me either**. Yeah, clearly, I had abandonment issues.

From the beginning of our marriage, our scenario was the perfect setting for some deep and hidden wounds in *both* of us to be brought to the surface. However, because we didn't know what to do about it, we just ended up creating an even bigger mess.

Even though I figured out quickly how I was feeling, I was convinced that it was the truth! I was tainted and unlovable, even to a loving God. I wish I could say that I quickly realized what was going on, received healing, and lived happily ever after, but I didn't, at least not right away. We lived that way for about eight years! I'm sure you know that much more damage can occur in that length of time, and it did. As if we didn't already have enough junk in our lives, we went on hurting one another, merely piling up the new wounds on top of the old ones, until we just couldn't take it anymore.

We had started to hate one another, and honestly, I didn't want to live. We were convinced that divorce was the only option. We had two children by then, and my husband had confidently promised them, for years, that he would *never, ever* leave us. Our family mantra was that divorce was absolutely not an option. However, we just couldn't take it any longer, and Roger left.

Once again, the message was confirmed to me that I was unlovable. Despite having a list of my husband's errors memorized, deep inside, I really believed that I was the problem. It was clear to me—I was worthless.

Finally, before our tenth anniversary, we did experience a miracle. God had been working even when we were convinced He wasn't. Through incredible circumstances, our marriage was saved. I'm happy to say that at the time of this writing, we have been married now for more than twenty-seven years. While the first eight years were incredibly difficult, the last nineteen have been great--not without challenges but still great amid the difficulties.

I learned so much about "committed" love, not only from Jesus, but from my husband. The fact that he came back home committed to making our marriage work showed me a side of love that I had never seen, and my relationship with Jesus flourished again.

I also learned so much about the precious Holy Spirit. He was and is legitimately the glue that holds us together. He never gave up on us. Even though it must have grieved Him to see us living that way, He never left our side. Through the years, He faithfully dug up things that were hidden in both of our hearts, and we co-operated. We grew and learned to walk in forgiveness. And, as time marched on, the Holy Spirit faithfully brought beauty out of the ashes.

Doubt, Rejection, Insecurity and so Much More

The years flew by like a calendar blowing in the wind. The painful hard work had paid off. We really had a new marriage. Of course, there were challenges, but they were the typical marital challenges, nothing like we had before. I was living my dream. I had the family I always wanted: an incredible husband and, by then, *four* amazing children.

I knew I was still a work in progress. Through the years, I had experienced deliverance and inner healing, and my life was so different from what it had been. God had indeed given me my heart's desires. The pain we had walked through was now being used to help others in crisis. Honestly, things were great.

I knew there were wounds from my father, and I was open and honest with God about them. I had long since forgiven my dad and kept in touch with him through the years. Even though it didn't happen that often, seeing him in person was still a challenge. I understood that he was a broken man, and I felt love and compassion toward him. Yet still, it was hard to be around him for very long.

He lived in Florida, and I lived in Colorado, so we kept in touch by phone. My dad wasn't into "meaningful conversations," so we mostly talked about cars, racing, and the weather. However, whenever he'd let me, I'd share with him what God had done for me, and I wasn't shy about telling him what God wanted to do for him.

It wasn't until we had been living in Colorado for more than six years that we traveled back to Florida. My father had not yet met our two youngest children. Since things had been going so well in our "phone relationship," I was looking forward to seeing him. However, just forty-five minutes into our visit, I wanted out of there! It wasn't that he had done anything wrong—it just all felt way too familiar. He still lived in similar living conditions as when I was young, so it felt as if I had been transported back in time. This not only surprised me, but it really disappointed me. I had wanted so badly to handle it better than I did.

A few months after we returned from that trip, our church was offering an intensive class on inner healing called, "Kairos." My heart has always been for the hurting, and I wanted to learn as much as I could, so my husband and I joined. Those classes came about at the perfect time! The Holy Spirit started working in my heart and revealed *new* things to me. There were so many incredible experiences with God during that time. One day in particular, I had a vision of Jesus and I sitting out in a field. I was lovingly leaning into Him and telling Him repeatedly, "I love you; I love you; I love you!" Before I could realize what was happening, He held up His finger to my lips, as if to gently request that I stop speaking. With kindness dripping from His words, He lovingly said to me, "Tammy, I know that you love Me...but you're not receiving **My** love."

What?

At first, I was surprised to hear that. It honestly didn't make any sense to me. Of course, I knew that God loved me! Sure, I struggled with doubt sometimes but only when things weren't going well. Intellectually, I knew that God loved me, as well as everyone else. Looking back now, I realize that if I would have been vulnerable enough to let someone open the secret parts of me, they would have found doubt, rejection, insecurity, and so much more. As much as I had changed, there was still more hidden in the deepest parts of me.

During one of the classes, they discussed the Trinity and how we relate or don't relate to any or all of the members of the Trinity: God, the Father; God, the Son; and God, the Holy Spirit. It was no surprise to me that I might have "daddy issues." However, I really didn't believe that I was relating them to God. After all, I had been through much inner healing and even deliverance. However, when they broke it down more specifically, the light bulb went off.

Let me start by saying, I'm not a theologian, and this is not a comprehensive study on the Trinity. However, if this matter has not been settled in your heart, I encourage you to study the Bible. The Bible teaches that there is one God, eternally existent in three persons: Father, Son, and Holy Spirit.

I know this subject can be overwhelming for some to wrap their mind around. When my children were young, I likened the Trinity to an egg. There are three distinct parts to an egg, but it's still one egg. *Each part of the egg has its own qualities and characteristics.* While they can be separated, it's still just one egg. When asking someone to give us an egg in our home, we don't usually say, please pass me the eggshell, the egg white, and the egg yolk. We just say, "Can you pass me an egg, please?" Like-wise, God has three parts, but He's one.

The speaker that day challenged us to look at how we relate to *each* of the members of the Trinity *individually*—to "separate" them, so to speak. It was through that exercise that the Holy Spirit revealed some startling things to me. It was then that I started to see that I might have a bigger problem with my view of *God as my Father* than I realized.

It was a painful process, but when I went below the obvious feelings of love and appreciation that I had for God the Father, I found out that I didn't trust Him. I thought I needed to perform for Him and that He could be a rigid and unpredictable God. How could I possibly think this about a God who had been *so* good to me?

The reason I hadn't realized that I thought these things deep in my heart was because I had been relating to Jesus all those years! He was the "Good Guy," the one who rescued me from God the Father's wrath. I had never really separated them before that day. I had heard through the years that our relationship with God is affected by our earthly fathers, but I honestly thought I had already worked through all of that. I didn't have time to process the revelation because that's when I received the letter, the one I had a feeling was coming.

3

FACING THE PAST

a short time before I visited my dad that summer, before I found out he was sick, I had begun to have dreams about my father passing away. This underlying thought sort of hung around taunting me. It was the most terrifying thought to me, not just on the normal level that we all would feel, but deeper because of all the pain I realized was still there.

That deep pain was buried so far down, and it was off limits. I had already, on numerous occasions, allowed the Holy Spirit to show me various wounds, but this one, oh no, this one was like an abyss that I could not go near or I might fall into it and never get out.

My stepmother's letter made it clear that things did not look good. Although they had divorced, she was still involved in my dad's life. She wanted me to know that he didn't have much time. All signs pointed to lung cancer, but he refused to do anything about it or tell anyone.

I felt as if someone punched me in the stomach with all their might. It was hard to breathe. I wanted to run so fast that maybe I'd disappear into another dimension. I just couldn't bear the thought of my dad dying. I knew the "right" thing would be to bring him to Colorado and take care of him, but I knew that would be the most difficult thing I would ever have to do. I was so double-minded. In one moment, I longed to hold him and love on him, but then the very next instant, I wanted to run as far away as I could.

I knew I had to go see him. However, an hour had been too much the last time I had visited. Knowing I needed moral support, my daughter, Hope, offered to go with me. We immediately made plans to go see him.

The First Visit

After speaking with my father and telling him of our upcoming visit, he still wouldn't tell me the whole truth. He never once mentioned that he had cancer, only that he was getting too old to take care of himself.

He said he had been considering the idea of living closer to my brothers who lived approximately five hours away from him. He had some concerns about moving to central Florida, so I offered to take him for a visit while I was there. It seemed like a perfect plan. He would get to check it out, and I'd get to see family that I hadn't seen in way too many years.

It was quite a surprise to see how much he had changed since I had just seen him months before. He had lost a lot of weight and needed help getting around. At the same time, he seemed better than my imagination had tortured me to believe. After staying a couple of days, my daughter and I drove him over to visit my brothers. It was so good to see everyone, but it was challenging, too. Being around my family was a reminder that the past really did happen!

The sad truth is that our family had not been around one another for many years. We didn't really know one another. We only knew the "old" versions of ourselves, so it was like walking into the past. My dad was going to stay with them for a day or two while my daughter and I were going to head back to visit my mother.

I hadn't made it to my mom's house more than an hour before I received the call that my dad had been rushed to the hospital. Everything changed very quickly after that. He couldn't leave the hospital for quite a while, and when he did, it was clear that he was not going to be able to go back to his trailer by himself. My youngest brother, Duane, teases me now and says that it was my intention all along to leave our Dad there. We laugh about it now, but God really did have a plan. Before my dad was released from the hospital, they had already retrieved and set up his trailer on my older brother David's property. This allowed him to feel like he was still in his own place, yet provided the opportunity for the family to be there to take care of him.

I am so proud of my brothers. They said yes to something that I know could not have been easy. This man they called dad had not "earned" the right to be taken care of, but they all laid down their lives to care for him in every way. Also, my sister-in-law, Sheila, accepted him with open arms as if he were her very own family. It was a beautiful thing they did.

I was back in Colorado and everyone there was taking such good care of him. He would take a turn for the worse and then rebound. I spoke to him often, but I wanted to see him again, so I made plans to stay for a week, something I had never done.

The Second Visit

I knew that this could be the last time I saw my father, and I was expecting God to do a miracle! As nervous as I was about the visit, my brother and sister-in-law made me feel so welcomed on my first visit that I was looking forward to seeing them again.

I couldn't believe my eyes when I saw him! He was down to skin and bones, literally. The first day that I sat with him, he was pretty drugged up. Watching him breathe was torturous. You could see that each breath was a chore, and it appeared as if each breath was going to be his last. We'd talk in between his naps, but for most of the day, I just watched him sleep off and on. I quietly and anxiously awaited a miracle, a moment that we would connect, really connect.

During one of his naps, as I intently watched his boney chest move up and down, I decided to sing a worship song. I just knew that this would usher God's presence into the camper and initiate that "moment of reconciliation." I began to sing, pouring out my worship to God quietly. All of the sudden, I heard this frustrated and confused voice snapping, "What's all that racket?"

"No worries, there's always tomorrow," I thought to myself. I was convinced that we were going to have *our moment*.

The next day, he seemed a little bit better. He was more awake and coherent. We even watched a race together. Unfortunately, there were little jabs and insults laced throughout the day's conversations. Somehow, they still had the power to sting, even though they weren't the first time I'd heard them. I knew that I only had a few more days, so I shook off the unkind remarks. Things were not turning out the way I had dreamed, but I continued to hold on to any shred of hope.

Throughout the week, my dad would occasionally allude to the reality of the situation. It was difficult for him to talk about what was happening. He was still in his camper, having returned from hospice, but he knew he wasn't getting better.

One afternoon, he started to address some of the details concerning his final wishes. He asked me to get him something from beneath the seat. I carried it over to him. It was a small but a heavy metal box. I didn't want to lay it on his lap because the skin on his legs was very thin and fragile, so I held it for him as he tried to open it. Before I could even realize what was happening, he instantly changed right before my eyes. Like a light switch being flipped from off to on, he immediately turned into the man I had known growing up.

As he screamed at me to get "the _____ out," I stood frozen, out of shock, but mostly out of fear. This man had put my mother in the hospital too many times for me to count. He had slammed my youngest brother against the wall, holding him by the throat. I had seen, countless times, what he was capable of. And, there I stood, within inches of his clenched fists. Despite being forty-five, I instantly became that terrified little girl, the one that I had been running from my entire life.

I wanted to run out like a scared little girl, but my legs wouldn't move! I was terrified. It was as if his anger fueled him, and he was no longer the frail, sick man I had been with all week. All of the sudden, he had strength. He wasn't short of breath as he yelled, "Get out of here before you give me a ___ing heart attack!"

Still, I was frozen. Something held me there, and before I could even think straight, I heard a voice, a loud voice, and it was coming out of **me**!

At blood-curdling volume, I screamed back, "DO NOT SPEAK TO ME LIKE THAT!" My body was shaking all over as I told him, at the top of my lungs and for the first time in my life, "I DO NOT DESERVE TO BE TREATED LIKE THIS!"

I don't know what I thought at that moment, but with all the adrenaline, he certainly had the strength to hit me. I didn't have time to think; it just happened. It was like a dam inside of me broke, and I couldn't hold back the flood. It was righteous anger, a realization that I was more valuable than the way he was treating me. I had reached my limit and decided I was not going to be a victim any longer.

I stood, not willing to budge a millimeter. For what seemed like minutes, there was dead silence between us. Then, I heard myself say, in a trembling voice, "Now Daddy, what can I do to help you?" I couldn't believe my ears. I never called my father, Daddy! Where did that come from?

When my legs finally started working again, I walked out of the camper so he wouldn't see me fall apart, and fall apart I did. At that moment, it still looked like a failure to me. I wanted loving, kind words to be spoken to my dad and from my dad. I wanted that "all healing moment" to occur between us.

The questions flew around inside my head, "What had I done to make him so mad? Why did he disapprove so much of me? Why could I never make him happy?

When I returned to the trailer, he acted as if nothing had happened. I sat down next to him so I could rub lotion on his sagging, bruised skin. As I continued to take care of him, the most beautiful picture unfolded. I thought about how God loves us, even when we aren't very lovable. Suddenly, loving the angry man in front of me took on a new meaning. Even though it was on a much smaller scale, I had been given a chance to imitate my Heavenly Father, and I decided it was a privilege.

Even though it was not the beautiful, fairytale moment that I had been longing for, God used it for good. For the first time in my life, I stood up to the scary, giant of a man that I called my father. I was empowered and terrified at the same time.

Saying Goodbye

It was the day before I was leaving, and I was starting to worry. Things had not gone the way I'd hoped, and I knew he didn't have much time. Hospice would check on him and tell us about the different stages that he was going through. Maybe it was the realization that my dad could be gone and I would never know, or perhaps it was my "newly found courage," but I decided I had to act.

I knew I was taking a big risk! My dad's answer could change everything either for the better or for worse. Still, I needed to know, so with all the courage I could muster, I let the previously unspoken words come tumbling out, "Dad, do you love me?"

"____ yeah! You know I do." He gruffly snapped.

Somehow, he must have known that I was looking for something—healing, closure, anything—because his next words shocked me!

"There, you feel better?" he sarcastically asked.

I couldn't believe my ears. Not many people get the chance that my dad was getting. Too many people die unexpectedly, leaving things unsaid, things that could change everything for the other person. I immediately stood up, ready to accept the worst-case scenario I had feared. If that was how he felt, then that was fine with me! How much more could I take?

Once again, determination rose inside of me, and I felt myself sit back down, right in front of him!

"NO! I do *not* feel better!" I firmly but calmly answered.

No child should ever have to ask a parent such a question, but I needed to know.

"Do you even like me?" I earnestly asked. I held my breath and waited in silence. Then, I saw his demeanor change just a little bit. Unlike the first time that he answered, his second response was less harsh.

He simply said, "I wouldn't change a thing."

I decided, "I'll take it!" Somehow, I knew that was the best my dad could give me. Whether he meant it or not, it didn't matter.

I am so happy to tell you that later that day, my dad accepted the Lord Jesus. He asked God to forgive him. His un-religious words developed into the most beautiful prayer I've ever heard, sincere and childlike. The week was not what I expected, not what I asked for, but I got the best that my broken father could give. And, most importantly, he surrendered his shattered life to Jesus Christ.

I wasn't there physically on the day that he passed into the arms of Jesus. I had already returned to Colorado. My brother called me though, and he held the phone to my dad's ear. They said that he had been showing signs of agitation, even though he was unconscious, but as I talked and prayed with him, they said he calmed down.

I had a hard time accepting that I wasn't with him when he departed for his new home. However, what brought me comfort was that Duane and Sheila were there, holding him like an innocent child as if he had never hurt any of us.

The Healing Continues

The next year was difficult. Grief seemed to take on flesh. It would chase me down and overwhelm me. At other times, it was a bit stealthier. It would sneak up on me, so unexpectedly and overtake me. At times, it was as if the air was literally being sucked right out of my chest.

Through that process, I kept remembering the words of my pastor. About the valley of the shadow of death, he said something like this, "Don't get stuck there. When you must walk through the valley, just keep walking." So, I did. When grief would overwhelm me, I would embrace it and grieve. Then, I'd get up and keep walking.

I've learned that as time goes on, grief runs slower and slower, and as time goes on, we make it to the other side. While we will never stop missing the loved ones we've said goodbye to, we don't have to allow grief to keep us imprisoned in the valley.

Although there was disappointment regarding my time with my dad, God helped me to see all the good that came out of it. Just a few short months before I found out that my dad was dying, I couldn't even sit with him for an hour, and I hadn't seen my siblings in years. Going through the loss together brought us closer than we ever were. Even though it's not as much as we'd like, because we live in different states, we are more a part of each other's lives now. I think we have a fresh appreciation for our family, even with all its dysfunction. I am grateful that we had the warning and the time to say goodbye to our father. My brothers tell me that they each had positive talks with him and that he was repentant.

While I never got to experience that "special" daddy moment that I wanted with my father, I did get to see the most important thing. I saw my father ask Jesus to forgive him and be his

Savior! The time I spent with him on the phone the day he went to heaven was so precious. I could literally feel the angels around me as I prayed with him. I know it brought him peace. I may not have been there physically, but that moment is one that I treasure beyond words. I'm so grateful that my brother and sister-in-love were with Him and loved him so beautifully.

During one of those moments, when grief successfully caught me, I fell to my knees and wept before God. I immediately sensed the Lord direct me to the song that was playing in the background. As I gave my attention to the words, I heard Big Daddy Weave's song, "Redeemed,"[1] and knew it was about my father. I found so much comfort in the words that spoke of my heavenly daddy's love for my earthly father. He had been so bound, and now he was so free.

As I sobbed on my bedroom floor, I could just imagine my dad singing that song. He was now redeemed. He was free from the chains that held him so tightly here on earth. He is happy and free for the first time in his life. He had experienced a terrible childhood himself, and rather than surrender that to God and walk in the freedom that God offered him here, he had refused it until the end of his life on earth. I am so thankful that God never gave up on him. He had done things that no one in the natural should be forgiven of, but that's God's specialty: forgiving.

That song is my dad's story. All his life, he had been told that he was unworthy. He knew the things he had done. He lived his entire life on this earth as his own enemy, and it prevented him from receiving and giving love.

I look forward to heaven for many reasons. One of which is that I will finally get to know the real man that I called my father. I will get to meet the man that God always intended him to be.

4

THE SHOWDOWN

*A*s my heart began to heal from the loss of my father, God brought back to my remembrance the vision I had when I was in the class. I could hear His words, "Tammy, I know you love Me, but you're not receiving My love." Even though I couldn't fully understand it, I could feel Him wooing me into the intimate but scary places that still needed to be healed.

If you had asked me, I would have **confidently** assured you that I believed God loved me. I really believed that I believed it! I was *very* aware of all that He had done for me. Of course He loved me. So, why did God say that I wasn't receiving His love?

It had been more than twenty-five years since that beautiful day I met Him, and I had been following Him with my whole heart. My life had sincerely been changed by Him. I knew the Bible stated that He loved me. As a matter of fact, I'd spent all those years telling others that Christ loved them! I had taught, given, evangelized, and ministered through the years. How could it be true that I was not receiving His love?

Did you notice above, everything was about me? It was all about what **I** was "doing." Again, God spoke very clearly to me that He knew I loved Him. That wasn't the problem! The problem was that I didn't know how much He loved me!

I had no idea what to do next. The only thing I knew for sure was that *if* it was true that I was not receiving His love, then I wanted to know why and what to do about it. So, I told Him that, tucked it away, and went about my life "doing good," but, God! He's marvelous! He's so patient. He's so *determined* to reveal His love to us that He lovingly waits for even more opportunities to get through to us, and that's what He did.

It was just a year or so later when I experienced what I can only describe as a "showdown." (I know, it's kind of ridiculous. We know who wins in a showdown with God, don't we?) Lexico.com describes the word *showdown* as the following: A final test or **confrontation intended to settle a dispute. Synonyms: confrontation**, deciding event, clash, face-off, moment of truth, crisis[1]

The catalyst, or final straw, for me, occurred during a prophetic conference. It had been a wonderful couple of days, and God was moving powerfully. However, on the last day, a gentleman stood up and shared his testimony of losing his fourteen-year-old boy. He said that he had been entirely *convinced* that his son was going to be healed. So, when his son died, he literally got on top of him and breathed life into his lifeless body, convinced still that his son was going to walk out of that hospital with him. Sadly, his son did not come back to life.

WHAT!!??

In just a matter of a second, my entire attitude and perspective changed. I went from having a fantastic time hearing

God's voice and enjoying His presence, to being shaken to my core with **anger**!

The following morning found me still so enraged with God that I couldn't even pray. I was lying in bed, brewing and stewing with anger. I was making a mental list of the things that I was upset with Him about when the mental picture turned into a vision. It caught me so off guard. When it was over, I sat up in bed, mouth wide-open, utterly shocked, not just by what I saw, but by the fact that He would show me *anything* when I was so furious with Him!

What I saw challenged me like nothing I had ever seen. I'm not going to share all of it, but in one part of the vision, I saw this massive drill, much like a super-sized auger. I could see that it was burrowing deep into a hole, and somehow, I knew the hole represented my life. I could see pebbles, and even boulders, that had been *previously* excavated from my life. However, as I continued to watch the rocks be torn apart and thrown from the hole, I saw the drill hit a new, much larger boulder. This one stretched nearly across the entire hole. As the powerful rotating blades hit the sizable rock, the drill stopped spinning. The next thing I heard was this tender yet authoritative voice say, "We can't go any deeper until we get this removed." At the time, I didn't know exactly what the boulder represented, but I fully understood that I wasn't going any further in my relationship with God until we removed it. That was my "rock bottom."

The collision of what I *wanted* to believe about God and what I *unconsciously thought* about God, blew up in my face. This deeply hidden trigger had made its way to the surface of my conscience once again, and I had a decision to make. I could ignore it or face it head-on. Finally, I chose the latter. I had to have a "conclusive settlement" of the issue: could I *really* trust God?

I knew it was time to lay all my cards on the table, face up—no more hiding and no more denying. I was so *tired* of making excuses for God and for why certain things weren't happening. I was so *tired* of being a "highly-functioning (yet dysfunctional) Christian." It wasn't like I had never been honest with God before; I had! But this, this was a new level of being "real." I was finally ready for Him to show me what I *really* thought and believed.

So, I started getting by myself, not for devotions, but for what, at first, were more like wrestling matches. The questions and accusations flew. Can I tell you something? God is NOT threatened by either. I think He welcomes them because, again, it's about the relationship! He wasn't threatened that I had my "dukes" up. Instead, He was so happy that I was no longer sweeping it all under the "religious rug."

I was so fed up that I was willing to lay down *everything* I had *ever* learned and thought I knew! I needed to know if what I currently had with God was all there was to this "Christian walk." I wondered if, maybe, I was asking for too much, because, honestly, I wanted more! I was not satisfied with my relationship with Him. All the things that I would say to others like, "It's not about religion; it's about a relationship," or "God wants to have an *intimate* relationship with you," were said more out of **faith** than actual **experience**. Sure, I had moments of intimacy through the years, but not consistently, not the way I longed for. I had no idea what I was going to come out believing, but I knew that whatever I came out with, it would be mine! I would own it. I decided that even if it involved me walking out with much less than what I already had, I was willing to go there.

I began to ask God to reveal ALL the beliefs that I had that might be distorted. I wanted to put *everything* that I held to be true on the altar. I wanted everything that could be hidden inside of me to be brought to light, and just like a Jack-in-the-Box toy that catches you off guard, it happened! My view of God as "Father" unexpectedly popped up. It was time to take a look at what I **really** thought about God as a **Father**. (I would challenge you, too, to do the same, even if you haven't walked through a past like mine. As a matter of fact, I think it's so helpful to look at *each* of the members of the Godhead *individually* because, believe it or not, we can relate to each of them differently, without even realizing it).

I think it's possible…no, I *know* it's possible, for even those with excellent parents to have distorted views of God as a Father. How many times have you heard someone say something like this, "God is punishing me with this disease?" Or perhaps it was something more like this, "God caused this traumatic event to test me." We've probably all heard things like this: "God took the child/baby because He *needed* him or her in heaven."

Please hear me when I say this. I understand that people who've said that to a grieving person meant well. I don't believe they *intended* to blame anyone. I'm sure their heart was in the right place, and they probably didn't know what to say. I, too, have blamed God and said similar things. However, I want you to see how that unintentional accusation can paint a negative picture of God without us even realizing it.

Can you imagine any of us as parents treating our children like that? We'd be put in jail for child abuse if we treated our kids that way. The first thought I would have as a parent when one of my kids was sick was, "I wish I could take their place." It was so painful to see one of my babies not well. Furthermore, if I wanted to see change in my children's behavior, I would **never** have considered putting a disease on one of my kids to teach them a "lesson." Yet, that is what many of us have believed about God the Father. Many of us have sung the words that He is a good Father all the while, unknowingly, *doubting* it within. We can quote scriptures and rebuke the devil until we're blue in the face, but we must get to the heart of the matter, and that is, "what does your *soul* believe?"

We also have an "accuser," or enemy. Satan desires to destroy us and our relationship with God. The Bible says he is the father of lies. You can bet he takes every opportunity to try to make us believe that God is not good. So, even if you had a healthy childhood, the struggles of life, Satan, and things we've heard from people, or even the pulpit, can often undermine the truth. It is entirely possible to have a dirty "God filter" without even realizing it.

As I allowed the Holy Spirit to continue to peel back the layers, I was *shocked* to see the thoughts that were lurking **deep** down below all the "pat" answers and religious beliefs. My heart and emotions (my soul) suddenly had a voice, and they were *not* in agreement with what I *said* I believed or even what I *thought* I believed!

Soul Beliefs Revealed

Most of us are aware that we are made up of three parts: body, soul, and spirit (1 Thessalonians 5:23). When we accept God's gift of salvation through Jesus Christ, our spirit man is born again. We become a new creation or a new creature (2 Corinthians 5:17). However, God does *not* give us a new body or a new soul at the moment of salvation. So, we start this new life with Jesus, our spirit made perfectly right with God, but we're left to deal with the *same* flesh and soul. I had heard hundreds of times that we should "rule and reign" over the body, but I hadn't heard *that* much taught about the soul. Of course, I knew it included the mind, will, and emotions. I also knew feelings weren't bad, but that they could be deceiving. I was well taught that I shouldn't live according to my emotions, but instead, by my spirit and according to the Word.

I also knew that it was vital that I renew my mind by reading the Bible. That made complete sense to me, so that's what I did. And I believe it did make a big difference in my life. Now let me say right here, I firmly believe the Bible is the Word of God! I know that it is alive and powerful. I believe that Jesus is the Word. However, with that said, the question I found myself asking after this showdown was, "Why, after ALL these years of loving God and reading His Word, was I not seeing the breakthrough and experiencing the intimacy I wanted?" I wondered why reading the Bible and quoting Scriptures had not *renewed my mind* in the specific areas that the Holy Spirit was now revealing. That's when God began to show me that I not only had a distorted view of Him as my Father, but I had *several* other negative soul beliefs!

Soul beliefs are the unseen messages that are written on our hearts. In other words, they are what our soul man has unknowingly concluded about God, life, ourselves, and others. They are usually the result of a deeply emotional (positive or negative) experience. While soul beliefs can be both positive or negative, we are going to discuss the damaging ones, the ones that hinder and even harm us.

One of the most important things for us to know about soul beliefs is that they can, and often are, in complete contrast to what we consciously believe! These destructive messages are subtle and even deceptive. You can live comfortably with them, without even realizing they are affecting you. They will often disguise themselves as wisdom, humility, or other religious characteristics. These conclusions can end up becoming judgments. Due to the beliefs lying below our conscious thinking and because most of us don't want to believe we view God negatively, it's critical that we examine our *behavior* and *attitudes*—and *not just the ones on the surface* but the ones that are hidden deep in our souls. Those are the ones that come out when we least expect it or when things aren't going the way we want them to or thought they would.

While you may be mostly successful at keeping the negative thoughts at bay, they somehow have a way of working themselves to the surface when something triggers them—things like disappointment, money problems, fear, rejection, etc. These patterns of thought aren't usually in the forefront of our conscience, but they easily slip out when we are under pressure or when we experience a challenging situation. It is usually only when the soul (the emotional part of us) is provoked that we can see that our reactions don't line up with what we *say we believe.*

We often blame these "ungodly" responses on things like being tired or "hangry." Of course, I'm not proclaiming that every single adverse reaction is a negative soul belief, but I am saying that if you see a common pattern, you should consider that possibility. When we blow off our reactions as being "the flesh" rather than realizing they are coming from the soul, we tend to ignore them. If we ignore them and only quote scriptures at them, we are simply pushing them back down into the wounded soul. I'm not saying the Bible doesn't help or that it's not powerful! **What I am saying is that we need healing so we can really believe what the Word tells us!** We must allow the Holy Spirit to identify the negative soul beliefs so that the emotional part of us can grab hold of God's promises. It is when these lies have been dealt with, that the power and truth of God's Word comes alive to our soul. We are not much of a threat to the enemy if we simply **know** the Scriptures. However, we are lethal weapons when we BELIEVE the Word with all our hearts, or our soul.

I would guess that most of us, if not all of us, at one point or another, have had the thought or feeling that God was angry, disappointed, or punishing us. Maybe you've questioned whether God is involved in your day to day life. Maybe God seems unpredictable to you or perhaps not interested in you at all. Do you secretly believe that God offers an abundance but delivers little? There are so many secret messages or beliefs about God that can be written on our soul without us realizing it. Whether what I heard from the pulpit confirmed my distorted beliefs or I misinterpreted what I heard, I discovered that I unknowingly had some seriously malformed opinions of God.

Perhaps you don't think God is the problem at all. Instead, maybe you believe that you simply need to pray more, work harder, or just "do more." We're going to talk about those lies, too.

Our unconscious, untrue, and preconceived ideas about God, others, and ourselves **will** influence us negatively. So, for the next several chapters, I'm going to expose some of the negative soul beliefs that were unknowingly affecting me. I'll also reveal how these undetected beliefs manifested in fear, shame, legalism, works, and more.

At the end of each chapter, there will be a "Challenge" section. I want to encourage you to not just skip over it because you don't think you're dealing with that specific issue. Instead, take some time to spend with the Holy Spirit. Ask the Spirit of Truth to reveal any preconceived ideas or false beliefs that you may have. He is a gentle, loving, and faithful Friend, who loves to speak to us.

Remember, we can pick up these beliefs in more than one way. While all our paths are unique; pain and disappointment are no respecter of persons. Pain is pain, no matter how it arrives. Besides, we all have the same enemy. So, I want to challenge you to ask the Holy Spirit to unearth any lies that you are *unknowingly* believing.

One good way to dig deeper is to look at your **responses** to different situations. Do you see a pattern in your life? Is there an issue that seems to keep coming up over and over? Or, are you merely dissatisfied with the level of intimacy that you have with God? This will require you to be honest and vulnerable. Sometimes, as Christians, we can be dishonest with others, but even more so with ourselves. We know the "right" things to say, and we know the "right" things to do. We know what we are supposed to believe! However, if there are some areas that you find yourself struggling, especially when things aren't going as well as you want them to, then I think it's worth an examination.

Please understand that I am not promoting a lifestyle of self-introspection. This is not about you looking for faults and weaknesses for the sake of beating yourself up! I did that for years. Believe me, that doesn't change you. Instead, I'm promoting a lifestyle of **intimacy** with the Holy Spirit so He has the freedom to reveal the lies you might be believing. This is about removing the stumbling blocks that are hindering you.

Jesus said He came to give us life abundantly (John 10:10). And, even though I was a committed, God-loving, Bible-believing Christian, I was not aware that I had some unde-tected negative soul beliefs that were hindering my intimacy and limiting breakthrough. I was, and I am, completely sold out to the Gospel, but I wanted more! We also know from Jeremiah 17:9 that our hearts cannot be fully trusted. So, it's possible to have some negative "scars" on our hearts that need to be healed. I firmly believe that the resulting freedom is worth a look. When we have the truth written on our souls, we can enter into freedom. We can revel in His good-ness. We can truly believe the Word of God and experience the intimacy with God that we were created for and so desire.

Once we've uncovered some common soul beliefs, we'll discuss how they are formed, what to do about them, and how to prevent them. If I were there with you, I'd take your hand or hold you and tell you that freedom is worth it. The things we fear the most are the giants that we must slay! When God started revealing the lies that I was believing, those venting sessions quickly morphed into worship! I say that with tears in my eyes because I don't know how He did it. He not only revealed the lies, but He started healing my hidden wounds, and those times turned into the most beautiful encounters that I have ever had.

Our Father desires to heal **all** our wounds. He does not want us limping through life. He clearly tells us that He came to give us abundant life. He wants us to know the *real* Him, without the filters and lies, so that we can experience true intimacy with the *Lover of our soul*. That brings me to this point: yes, He loves our soul, even when it's broken and messy. However, He doesn't want it to stay that way.

PRAYER

Holy Spirit,

I want to experience the fullness of all that You have for me. If there are things in my life that are preventing me from really knowing and receiving Your love, then I want them dealt with and gone. If there are things that I unconsciously believe that are contrary to Your truths, I ask You to shine a light on them. I want to know YOU, not the God that I've been led to think You are! I want to walk in the revelation of Your relentless love.

I want an intimate relationship with You, so if there is more to this "Christian walk" than what I've been experiencing, I want it! I don't want to miss out on anything You've made available.

You are the initiator of this relationship. You chased me down, even when I wanted nothing to do with You. You gave everything so I could be forgiven and we could have a relationship. So, I ask You to reveal anything that could be secretly hindering me from knowing You more. Expose every negative, untrue soul belief that I might have. I want to hear directly from YOU. I want to know what You think so I lay all my preconceived ideas on the altar, and I ask You to resurrect the truth and only the truth. In the precious name of Jesus, I pray. Amen.

PART II

WHAT WE BELIEVE DETERMINES HOW WE BEHAVE

5

I DON'T TRUST YOU?

UNCOVERING HIDDEN SOUL BELIEFS

*A*s a relatively new believer, I remember hearing a particularly tragic story on the radio. It's long, so I'll summarize it by saying that this Christian man ended up losing his wife and child in such a senseless, tragic way.

I'm sure we can all relate to this. We've heard the heart-wrenching stories that our minds simply cannot comprehend. As I listened to this man's story, the arrows of the enemy began piercing my mind and my heart. I quickly began asking, "How could a good God let that happen to a family that loved and served Him?"

Through the years, that story and another more personal one went deep enough to penetrate my heart and left me with a scar. It wasn't a visible or noticeable scar, but it affected my inner, unrealized thinking. ***I wasn't sure I could trust God!***

Even though I had experienced His goodness, deep in my subconscious, I didn't know if I was safe with Him. In addition, Satan was right there to try to convince me that God could not be trusted. I'm sure it's understandable, given my childhood, that I would grow up without a sense of security. When the one you are supposed to trust the most or the one who is supposed to keep you safe is the reason you are harmed, you don't develop a platform of safety to stand on. When violence occurs at the hand of the one that is supposed to keep you safe, it destroys the **foundation** of security that is supposed to be established by your parents. However, with that said, you don't have to have experienced an abusive childhood to struggle with trusting God. Disappointment and pain have a way of leaving their scars on us, too.

According to vocabulary.com, one definition of the word cornerstone is **the fundamental assumptions from which something is begun or developed or calculated or explained.**[1] Think about that. The things you and I have experienced or believed are the fundamental beliefs from which everything else springs. No wonder we need God to tear down our broken foundations and renew our minds.

As a little girl, being alone in very unsafe places, broken promises, lack of the necessary provisions, and violence were my fundamental assumptions. They were all I knew and had punctured a hole in my heart. My dad had let me down in more ways than I could count. He was the source of much of my pain. So, when it even *remotely* looked like God failed me, it was easy for me to blame God, the Father. After all, my beliefs and assumptions had been developed to not expect to be cared for and not to expect unconditional love.

The result? FEAR, FEAR, and more FEAR!

One of the most prominent scars that it left on my heart was that when I heard about a tragic loss, or tragedy in general, I would take it to heart and be affected immensely! When I heard painful stories, I immediately experienced fear. I would relate to it and "feel" it in such a real way. I know we all feel sad when we hear about a loss or painful situation, but for me, it was abnormal. It became **"an all too real possibility."**

As one who experienced so much pain growing up, it didn't take much for me to imagine the worst. Even though I was now devouring the Word of God, my soul was still more accustomed to pain, loss, and sadness than joy and peace. So, if we were experiencing a lapse in chaos, I would get nervous, waiting for the other shoe to drop. Loss and pain were my companions. The problem was, when I got saved, it took a long time to unfriend them. As I grew in my relationship with Jesus, I experienced some freedom. The terror from the phone ringing at night improved. And, after years of some normalcy, I thought that I had changed considerably.

However, there was still some residual, hidden deep in the crevices of my soul. One definition of "residual" from Merriam-Webster is **an internal aftereffect of experience or activity that influences later behavior.**[2] The internal aftereffect that was controlling my life was the fear of losing my husband and children, but, if I'm honest, that wasn't the only fear. For you, it might be a fear of failure, divorce, bankruptcy, disease, etc.

So, when I heard about other Christians experiencing that kind of loss, the soul belief of distrust was triggered. It felt as if Satan was dragging me around by the neck, pointing out the horrible catastrophes and possibilities and telling me that I was next! If it happened to others, it could happen to me! Remember, I already knew loss and disappointment very well. They were very familiar to me.

I will be honest and tell you that this fear still tries to knock on my door. The great news, however, is that it's not *controlling* me. For way too many years, I opened the door and let it right in. It controlled my way of thinking, acting, and living. When the knock comes to my door now, I don't answer it! I stand against it.

We all know that on this side of heaven, we will experience loss. After all, until the Lord's return, each of us will come to the end of our time here on earth. The lie, though, is that God tests us or sets us up, or even punishes us with loss, pain, or sickness.

I want to tell you that our Father is not the author of loss. He is not the author of sickness. He does not punish or test us with misfortune or tragedy. Do those things happen? Of course. We know they do. However, God is not the one dispensing them.

The Bible is clear about who comes to kill, steal, and destroy. It's the devil, not God. John 10:10 (AMP) says: "The **thief** comes *only* in order to steal and kill and destroy. (Jesus said) **I** came that they may have and enjoy life, and have it in abundance (to the full, till it overflows.)" As clear as those verses are, so many of us get that confused. We tend to blame God for the bad things that happen. Reading one verse further, it says, "**I** am the **Good Shepherd**. The Good Shepherd risks and lays down His (own) life for the sheep."

If you're like me, I heard these scriptures many, many times, but it must have just gone in one ear and out the other because I **unconsciously** still blamed God! Without even realizing, I was *not* convinced that He was good. I thought He *could* be good, but I questioned whether He was good all the time. I saw Him through the distorted lens of my own broken father. Back in the nineties, I heard messages that seemed to convey the idea that difficulties, pain, and sorrow somehow equated to holiness. It meant you were "doing something" for God.

To be completely honest, *inwardly*, I thought He was unpredictable. I would hear it preached that God was good, but then I'd hear other things that seemed to insinuate the opposite. I can see now that the lines were very blurry for me. I blamed what the *enemy* did (steal, kill, and destroy) on God, who gives abundant life. I would let the *circumstances* dictate to me my view of God. In other words, I permitted circumstances to convince me that God was not who He said He was. I did not realize it at the time, but I unconsciously thought that God punished us with sickness, tragedy, and difficulties. I can remember these words coming out of my mouth more than once, "God, I just can't take any more of Your testing!" Now, please remember, these thoughts **only** came out during challenges. They were not my every day, conscious thoughts. I loved God, and I was a committed believer. These secret thoughts were how I viewed Him, and I didn't even realize it.

How many times have you heard people say something like this— "Don't pray for patience or God will set up opportunities for you to be tested in that area"—? I'm sorry, but that paints a terrible picture of God for *me*. Think about that. Here you are, asking for something good, a fruit of the spirit which the Holy Spirit GIVES (see Galatians 5:22-23), only to be met with a God Who purposely "sets you up?" I'm *not* saying that God won't correct you or me in an area of our lives that He wants to see change. However, the picture that it **subliminally** painted for me was one of a harsh drill sergeant, secretly taking pleasure in challenging me and pushing me to my limit.

Maybe it was because of the negative view established by my father, but there were so many seemingly innocent comments that portrayed a negative picture of God to me. I don't think I'm the only one who has struggled with these types of thoughts. I suspect that many of us have found ourselves doubting His goodness and love because it is implied that God is uncaring, distant, harsh, impossible to please, or even the source of pain and suffering. Even if you haven't heard that implied from the pulpit, I guarantee you that Satan loves to hurl those types of lies at us. Until God revealed the negative soul belief that had been carved on my soul, it never dawned on me that when I went through difficult seasons, maybe my Father was, instead, lovingly weeping and holding me.

Would the Real God Stand Up?

When I was young there was this show called, "To Tell the Truth." I don't remember all the details except that they would have three people claiming to be the same person. The contestants would ask questions to try to figure out who was the "real" person that they were all *claiming* to be. The thing that stands out in my mind is when the host would ask the question, "Would the 'real' so-and-so stand up." Through the years, I had that same question run through my mind. "Would the real God stand up?" **I just wanted to know which version of God I could actually have.**

Like the contestants from the show, I would vacillate, trying to "guess" who the real God was. What I saw didn't line up with His description. I heard God wanted intimacy with us, but much of the time I felt there was an invisible barrier between us. I read that He was a healer, but I rarely saw someone healed. I heard that He wanted to be involved in our lives, so why was I often left feeling so ignored by Him? Why was I so hungry for more? I'll tell you why. There were invisible scars on my soul that were so thick that it was hard for God's love and truths to penetrate. It was a hit or miss type of relationship. Sometimes it made its way into my heart, and sometimes it didn't. And when it didn't, I simply relied on my obedience and determination.

I want to tell you that there is so much more. God is so incredibly kind, and when we believe things about Him that are not true, our relationships with Him, others, and ourselves suffer. The truth is, God is astonishingly good! Look at these verses:

> For You, O Lord, are good, and ready to forgive (our trespasses, sending them away, letting them go completely and forever); and you are abundant in mercy and lovingkindness to all those who call upon You.
>
> —Psalm 86:5, AMP

> The Lord is good to **all**, and His tender mercies are over all His works (the entirety of things created).
>
> —Psalm 86:5, AMP

> You are good, and what you do is good; teach me your decrees.
>
> —Psalm 119:68, NIV

I could go on and on. There are so many scriptures that tell us how good God is. I can't tell you how many times I read those and other similar scriptures and still didn't realize that I *doubted* His goodness.

So, does knowing the scriptures, or even memorizing them, mean you *assuredly* believe God is good and that you trust Him? Does singing out the worship songs wholeheartedly mean you completely agree with them? I don't think so, at least not always. I believe with all my heart, had you asked me back then, that I could have honestly said to you that I wholeheartedly believed what the Bible said. However, my fears, my inner thought life, and my insecurities didn't agree with my head! I wanted to believe that I believed them, but the secret place of my heart and my emotions were full of doubt. When God showed me that I had hidden, negative soul beliefs, I was shocked. I had been in the Word for years. How could there be such a contradiction of what my soul believed and what I thought I believed?

I respectfully say that I suspect that a lot of us Christians say and sing one thing and, yet, have undetected soul beliefs that do not match what comes out of our mouths. I don't say that to be mean or judgmental. I cannot stress enough to you that I was **not** aware that I thought these things. I was successfully serving in the church and "even making a difference in others' lives." It's possible to have these types of damaging beliefs and not even be aware of it.

Because of this, I truly believe that freedom starts with exposing the lies. If we aren't even aware that we have distorted views of The Father, Jesus, or Holy Spirit, we can continue to live defeated lives, missing out on the victory and intimacy that God offers us.

We live in a fallen world, and we have a real enemy. However, *knowing* that my loving Father is *not* the source of that, allows me to walk more intimately with Him. **Knowing** this has made a major difference for me. How in the world can I experience *real* intimacy with someone that I can't trust? While some struggle to believe that God is going to protect them or their loved ones, others battle trusting God for provision. There are so many ways that we can doubt God's faithfulness or trustworthiness. The key is to recognize those areas and give them to Him because He wants to heal us. He wants us to know who He REALLY is!

I heard someone say, "When we experience fear, we have two choices, we either trust or try to take control. If we don't think God is good, we'll lean toward the latter.

CHALLENGE

Do you find yourself dealing with fear in **any** area on a consistent basis? With love and compassion I tell you, it's certain that you are struggling to trust God in that area. I don't say that lightly. I understand, but God wants to heal that wound! He doesn't want us in bondage to anything. Our God has shown Himself strong on our behalf, and He wants to remove the lies that are hindering our relationship.

One of those hindrances is disappointment. Delayed or unfulfilled promises and broken dreams can undermine our trust in God. If we're not careful, we can let those dashed hopes create a wedge between us and God, often, without us even realizing it. This can make it difficult to trust Him again. Feeling like God didn't come through can make trusting God more challenging the next time. This can often cause us to want to "be in control" rather than truly releasing it and trusting the results to Him. You might be saying, "I'm not dealing with fear." However, if there are any areas where you "take over," rather than trusting God to be in control, then I would challenge you to find out why. Are you more confident in *your* efforts than you are in God's? Whether we struggle with fear or control, the roots can always be traced back to our soul's view of God.

- Do you think God can be a bit unpredictable?
- Does God ever seem distant or unsympathetic?
- Do you think God is just too busy for you or that you are unimportant to Him?
- Do you struggle with fear?
- Is it hard to trust God with your dreams?
- Do you feel like God has let you down time after time?
- Have you ever thought that God is out to get you or that He is "setting you up?"
- Have you ever felt like God was unfaithful with His promises to you or someone you know?

If so, my heart breaks for you. I know what it's like to struggle with distrust and fear. However, I promise you, there is freedom! Jesus's blood paid for it. Your perfect heavenly Father wants to heal you so you can fully embrace His truth, but that begins with your honesty and willingness to get these things out into the open.

It is Satan who wants to steal our hope, our joy, and our trust. He wants to fill our lives with disappointment and fear! Proverbs 13:12 says: "Hope deferred makes the heart sick: **but** when the desire comes, it is a tree of life" (AKJV).

Your Father's love is greater than any painful, disappointing experience! And, that healing begins in the presence of Your loving Father.

PRAYER

Abba (Father),

The Bible says that You want an intimate relationship with me. Pain, disappointments, and fear have tried to be my companions and crowd You out. I ask You to go deep and heal every wound. Show me when I started believing the lie that I am not safe with You or that I can't trust You. If there are any undetected, incorrect views that I have of You or any lies that I believe, I ask You to bring them into the light. I want to know the truth!

*Forgive me for blaming You. I ask You to reveal and heal the doubts and disappointments. I want to walk confidently and intimately with You. You are a perfect Father, and You are for me and not against me. The Bible is clear that the enemy comes to kill, steal and destroy, but **You** came to save me and to give me abundant life. I break the power of fear. I refuse to get into agreement with fear because fear makes me believe things that aren't true!*

*I don't want to say, "You are good," with just my lips; I want to **know** it unwaveringly. I want to know it in my soul. Thank You for revealing the truth to me. In the name of Your precious Son, I pray. Amen.*

I would encourage you to now spend some time in His presence, not to pray, but to listen. Worship Him with your presence. Listen, inwardly, for Him to speak to you. Let Him show
you the truth. He truly is crazy about you!

6

I HAVE TO BE GOOD ENOUGH?

DEALING WITH LEGALISM AND PERFORMANCE

*S*adly, believing that I wasn't *really* safe with God wasn't the only lie that needed to be exposed. From the moment I started walking with Jesus, I wanted all my sins gone! I gave up everything I thought was sin and even things that weren't. I tried to do everything right. I also wanted to try to make everyone else do everything right. By the way, I don't recommend that.

I think we can become performance-based for many reasons. Regardless of the "why," I think way too many of us struggle with this. Really, it's so prevalent in our society to unknowingly try to get our worth from what we do.

What I have experienced, and have seen in others' lives, is that we forget that we were saved by grace, or maybe we never really understood it. We hear it over and over, but then we unconsciously make it about something else—things like legalism, works, or performance. I really believe that living like that interferes with having an *intimate relationship* with God.

For me, a clear picture had been painted. When I didn't do something "right" in my father or my first stepfather's eyes, I suffered the consequences. I heard, "You can't earn God's love," a thousand times or more. I knew it in my head but not in my heart. Deep in my soul, hidden under many other things, I concluded that God was just too hard to please. Honestly, I sort of lived in a way that just expected His sudden disapproval and punishment.

My dad was angry all the time. Seriously, I can only recall a few times when he wasn't angry. Even when he was not actively raging in a fit, he just lived in a state of anger. On the few occasions where he was having fun, he would change in the blink of an eye.

It was very easy for me to conclude—*without even realizing it*—that I had to try to be perfect for my earthly father. However, if you would have told me I was projecting the same dread or fear of sudden and unexpected wrath onto God, I would not have believed you for a second. It really was the furthest thought from my cognizant thinking. I truly thought that I had already dealt with those lies. What I didn't know was that my soul did feel that way. It made me live with an invisible check-list of yes's and no's. Just like when I was a little girl, I was constantly and painfully aware of my actions. I wanted God's approval so badly. And, because I didn't realize that I *already* had it, I fell headfirst into legalism and performance.

Legalism

When you are legalistic with yourself, you can bet you're legalistic with others. Legalism showed up everywhere. With my first two kids, I was more concerned with teaching my children how to "be good Christians and stay away from sin" than introducing them to the most awe-inspiring LOVE they'd ever know. I know we need to be balanced, and we need to teach our children why and how to make good choices, but for much of their foundation, I lived in *fear* that they would "sin." It was out of balance for me. Yes, I assured them that God loved them, but I unconsciously concentrated so heavily on what they shouldn't do and not on the One who loved them and was crazy about them. The harsh truth is, I unknowingly "taught" them, without wanting or trying to, what I **really** thought about God! Ouch! In other words, my words said, "God's love is unconditional," but I didn't live that way. How could I teach them about this relentless, passionate, loving God when I didn't know Him to be that way?

It showed up with my husband, too. In my eyes, my convictions needed to be his convictions, because after all, mine were right. (I know it's sad, but that's what I thought). Unfortunately, that developed into a mommy-son relationship. Let me confidently tell you, that doesn't work!

Of course, it showed up in my relationship with God, too. Deep in my heart I perceived that God **could** be harsh and difficult to please. I could do many things "right" and still feel like it wasn't enough. Notice that I said "could" be harsh. I would never have said with my lips that God **was** harsh because that would have been so contrary to what the Word says. It took me years to realize that I unconsciously viewed Jesus as the gentle and kind One, the One that loved me enough to die for me. However, God…well, He was the stern Father in heaven, keeping an eye on me. I unconsciously thought, "If I behave, God the Father will basically tolerate me for Jesus' sake." So, when things weren't going well or I faced a challenge, I just assumed that the Father must be mad at me or He wanted to teach me a lesson.

That's just not true! It was God, your **Father**, who loved you SO MUCH that **HE** came **through** Jesus. Jesus told us in John 14:9 that if we saw Him, then we had seen the Father. Colossians 1:15 says, "He is the divine portrait, **the true likeness of the invisible God**, and the firstborn Heir of all creation." (TPT). Hebrews 1:3 also tells us that Jesus is the exact representation of God's nature. So, how did Jesus treat people when He was here? Well, there you go—you've now seen the Father's nature. There is no "good-cop/bad-cop" scenario with God. Therefore, the Father doesn't just "tolerate" you for Jesus' sake; He loves you just like Jesus does. His desire for you was so great that He came to rescue you.

What breaks my heart is that for many years, I and many others, have been misled to believe things about our amazingly kind Father that are contrary to the Bible and Who He really is. Whether it's intentional or simply implied, God is often accused of being harsh, uncaring, distant, impossible to please, and even the source of pain and suffering. No wonder so many of us have found ourselves doubting His goodness and love. Do you know whose nature is harsh, uncaring, and the source of pain and suffering? It's Satan's.

While Jesus came to give us life, it is the devil that tries to take our lives. It is the enemy's great pleasure and intent that you distrust and blame God. It has always been his goal to try to get us to doubt God's motives. The first case of this was in the Garden of Eden. Satan planted the seed of doubt that caused Eve to question God's goodness, and he's been doing it ever since. The truth is, we never see in the Bible Jesus withholding healing from anyone because they needed to "grow" or be "taught a lesson." I knew this in my head, but somehow, my soul wasn't convinced.

These kinds of soul beliefs about God's character unconsciously prevent intimacy and hinder breakthrough. I don't know about you, but when I was faced with many "tests and trials" and thought God was to blame, it didn't cause me to grow closer to Him, instead many times, it made me withdraw or become angry. Why would anyone want to run to the one that they think is causing the pain? They wouldn't, but when that soul belief has been exposed and healed, it allows you to run to the One from whom your help comes from.

As you can imagine, this deep-seated belief absolutely interfered with my ability to receive God's unconditional love. In my mind I said He was kind, but unconsciously I doubted that. Because my view of His nature was wrong, I certainly wasn't convinced that His love was unconditional. I would have said it was, but I didn't live like it.

Performance

I wanted to be the best daughter in the world. I wanted to serve God and do everything He asked me to do. While my heart was right, my motives were contaminated. I was trying to earn His love and avoid His judgment. I unconsciously believed that I had to be perfect for God to love me or not be mad at me. Sadly, I had transferred my performance-based beliefs from my dad right over to God the Father. At that time, I would have argued with you until I had no breath left. I honestly didn't believe that I was doing that. It was when I separated God the Father from Jesus that I could see that I actually had two different views of them.

Performance was at the very core of who I was. I worked so hard at everything, especially trying to be good and pleasing to the Lord. I assure you, there is no joy in that! I felt like I was jumping through *moving* hoops. While I think that it's great to have an excellent work ethic; it's not good if you're trying to get your self-worth from what and how you do something instead of *who you are.*

The problem is that if **who** you think you are is unlovable, then you're not going to want to just **be** who you are because you feel that who you are is unacceptable. The painful messages accumulate, and the next thing you know, you don't really need anyone else to tell you how bad you are. You've heard the negative content enough that you can parrot it back to yourself, verbatim. And, without even realizing it, you've taken over their job and become your own worst enemy.

My father never made me feel like he liked me. He acted like I was a disappointment to him. It felt like he was always pointing out the things that he didn't like. I can only remember two times in my life when my father said something semi-life-giving to me instead of telling me what he didn't like about me. I'm sure that was not his intention. He probably never even realized what he was doing. He was a hurting man, hurting others.

As a parent myself, I've made that mistake, too. Without even realizing it, I would tell my children something that I thought was "helping" them, but it came across in an unfavorable way. Maybe the words themselves weren't invalidating or hurtful, but to them they came across as if they were. Of course we know that the enemy will twist those words around and try to beat all of us over the head with them.

To this day, I still want to do what's right. The difference though is that now I know that His love for me is not dependent on what I do or don't do. I cannot make Him love me any more than He does! (I can't say that enough.) And now, I **really** believe it. It was St. Augustine that said, "By loving us, God makes us lovable."[1] So when I see areas in my life that I want to change, rather than beat myself up and pull further from my Father, I lean in. I've learned that it is in His **loving presence** that true change occurs. Now that I know how much He loves me, I don't have to pull away. I can run into His arms with all my junk, knowing that He is the One that can change me.

So, if God loved you and I so much that while we were deep in our sin, He came to rescue us, then why do we decide that, now that we have been reconciled to Him, we have to perform to **keep** His love?

Unadulterated Grace

I think God loves us more than He hates our sin. Did you just shudder when I said that? There was a time that I would have been very concerned if I heard someone say that. Please, just hear me out.

Why do we, as parents, have family rules? Because we **LOVE** our children and we want the best for them. When they break one, do we stop loving them? Absolutely not! What makes us think that we are better parents than God, our Father?

Why do you think God has "rules?" Because He **LOVES** us and knows what's best for us! When He tells us not to commit adultery, it's **not** because He can't **love** us any longer *if* we do commit adultery. He knows the horrible consequences of adultery and doesn't want that for us. He knows that it destroys trust, breaks hearts, ruins families, spreads diseases, and so much more. For the same reasons that we teach our children not to lie, steal, commit adultery, etc., God tells us what we shouldn't do. It's for *our* benefit.

So, am I saying that God doesn't require righteousness? Actually, I'm saying the complete opposite! God is holy, and **legally** speaking our sin had to be punished. It had to be dealt with. Since righteousness **is** required, Jesus stepped in and did what we couldn't. It is through HIS life, death, and resurrection that we are given the *legal right* to *be* right with the Father. He did what we couldn't do! It's not about being good enough for Him to love or clean enough for Him to tolerate— It's about stepping into all that **He** has made available to us. He literally clothes or covers us with His robe of righteousness, but so many of us don't know how to really receive that. It's like we unknowingly rip off the robe and like a two-year old shout, "Look Daddy, I can do it all by myself."

Obedience is good! No doubt about it. However, it is NOT what puts us in right standing with God. Instead, it's *Christ's* obedience that did that for us! (Romans 5:19). When that becomes a reality, you start to *enjoy* your relationship with Him. One of our pastors said something like this, "If you aren't sure what kind of God you are going to encounter, you'll probably avoid going to Him." That is so true! It is when we really see Him for who He is that we can come boldly before the throne of grace (Hebrews 4:16). *The Passion Translation* puts it like this, "So now we come freely and boldly to where love is enthroned, to receive mercy's kiss and discover the grace we urgently need to strengthen us in our time of weakness."

Now, I know there may be some that are concerned that I'm taking God's grace for granted. You might be thinking that people who get all "wrapped up in God's love" tend to use it as an excuse for sinful behavior. How do I know that? Confession time: I used to think like that. I secretly assumed that the people who were "all about love" were more tolerant of sin! Now that I've encountered *God's love for me* rather than just *my love for Him,* I believe with all my heart that it's just the opposite.

I love the Church! She is Jesus' beautiful bride, and He intensely loves her. So I'm not bashing the church when I say this, but I think there has been this unspoken fear in some congregations that if we teach or preach God's love too much that it will cause people to live sinful lives. In other words, they will take His love for granted and live as if they can just do anything they want.

I have such love and respect for pastors. They serve in such selfless ways! They also see and hear things from their congregation that can, if they are not careful, cause them to become cynical. My husband and I, having been marriage mentors/counselors for years, can understand to a *small* degree what pastors can go through when they hear what goes on behind closed doors. While I won't argue with you, what we see all dressed up on Sunday isn't always the way it really is. I would even go so far as to say that there are "wolves" dressed up in "sheep's" clothing.

With all that said, I still wonder: is much of what people are struggling with because they have not understood—for *themselves*—how deeply loved they are? I must wonder, is it because they went from one form of bondage to another? Have they fallen into the hands of a loving God, or the hands of a seemingly harsh and demanding God?

I had been thinking about this for a few weeks, when one day I heard the Lord say to me, "Tammy, how do you act with your husband when you don't feel loved by him? I immediately knew the answer, "Ugly." When I feel important, protected, and loved by my husband, it is so much easier to put him first and be kind, considerate, and respectful of him. When I feel neglected or insignificant to him, it is so much harder to do the right thing. When I am uncertain of his love, my behavior isn't always what I want it to be. Sure, I'm responsible for my behavior, regardless of what my husband does or does not do. That's true. However, I will tell you, for sure, it is so much easier to "do the right thing" when I feel loved by him. His love has a positive effect on me.

I think that's how we can behave with God, without even realizing it. If we feel unloved, neglected, unprotected, or insignificant to Him, I think it can easily affect our behavior and our choices. When our relationship isn't healthy—because it's based on something other than what HE did—it influences everything. I think many of us, when we don't realize how much God loves us, tend to either choose sin or legalism. Either way, both hinder intimacy with God.

I honestly believe that when we come face to face with His unconditional love, it changes us! When I'm thoroughly convinced that He is crazy about me, it affects my behavior in a positive way. When I'm full of His love, I want to do what is right. In other words, I don't want to act ugly. You may be asking, "Is it really that easy?" I honestly believe it is. Romans 2:4 says it is His kindness that leads us to repentance. When we encounter HIS love for us, our love for Him explodes!

I don't want to come across as a know-it-all. I don't know what it's like to be addicted to drugs or porn. If you struggle with any of those, my heart goes out to you. I do know, however, what it's like to be bound! I can also tell you, unequivocally, that bondage is bondage. However, *every* chain is breakable! The same loving Father that sets us free from fear, pride, or rejection sets us free from porn, drugs, or any other bondage. I don't want you to think that your sin is just too big, or too awful for God to forgive and set you free. His **love** for **you** is greater than what you're struggling with!

Not receiving God's love *individually* can cause us to not only live a destructive life, but an empty one. For example, I mentioned before that when I accepted Jesus as my Savior, I worked so hard at eliminating from my life all the *"bad things."* In other words, "Yay for me! I wasn't fornicating, stealing, etc. Woohoo!" However, I was still in bondage! I was not living the life that Jesus died for me to live. When I realize how much He loves me, I mean when I REALLY encounter His love, I just don't want to do those things. If I do something wrong, I'm quicker to repent. It is His goodness and kindness that leads me to repentance (Romans 2:4). Before that, it was just me striving, unhappily I might add, to gain His love and approval. There was no intimacy, just performance.

He adores **me** even when I blow it and disrespect my husband. He adores **me** even if I yell at my children. He adores **me** even if I *sin,* because I have been made righteous.

Notice that I **didn't** say He adores what I do! However, He does adore, or intensely loves, me! That truth doesn't make me think that I can just keep doing whatever I want and not experience consequences.

Let's take the example of me disrespecting my husband. If I continue to do that, which is wrong, my relationship with him will be affected negatively. That is a result of *my* choice, not God punishing me. My negative actions will produce negative results. If my Father needs to discipline me, it will be done in love and for my good.

What I've discovered is that it's His kindness, love, and grace that makes me NOT want to do those things. When I blow it, I can come boldly before Him to receive His love and forgiveness. As a matter of fact, the closer I get to God and the more intimate we are, the more He will show me things that He would like to see removed from my life. That's a beautiful thing! I had always viewed Him more like a mean, holy God with a measuring stick. I now know that He is a loving Father who wants the best for me.

For too long I assumed that He only loved me when I was doing everything as "right" as I could. I acted as if my new behavior needed to be good enough to **repay** God for what Jesus had done. His love is unconditional, but I put **my** own conditions on it. I did not comprehend how much God loved *me,* so I tried to "earn" it by obeying and performing. Romans 3:20 says: "Therefore **no one** will be justified in His sight by works of the Law. For the Law merely brings awareness of sin." It's a vicious cycle. I just could not reach the standard of holiness on my own. You see, God is the only One who can change us. We can do everything that we think we're supposed to do and "not do," everything we're told not to do, and still have a sinful heart. Jesus did for us what the Law could not!

Deep in my heart I think I believed that He loved my "good" *behavior* more than He actually loved me. The problem with this kind of thinking is that it's counterproductive. The reason I say that is because the *lie* that you have to "earn it" will always stand in the way of you being in complete **AWE** of God's amazing grace! In other words, if you are "trying to earn" or even "trying to pay Him back," you will never *experience* the goodness and kindness of His **pure grace**. You won't experience the generosity of His undeserving love. When you know His grace, you don't want to take it for granted or abuse it.

Not only is it hard to have an intimate relationship with someone that you don't fully trust, it's also equally difficult to have a *close* relationship with someone that you must perform for. Each one of us wants to be fully loved and accepted for just being us. We want someone to think we are extraordinary and to accept us just as we are. We want someone to love us for *who we are*, not only for what we can do for them.

Imagine for a minute that your spouse **only** loves you because you cook for them, clean for them and take care of them; or maybe it's only because you provide for them. What happens if you are ever unable to do those things for them? They wouldn't love you anymore.

How silly for us to think that God's love is that shallow and selfish. Let's face it, our performance can change from one day to the next. What kind of God would He be if His love was that fickle? It's not!

His love is the kind that chased us down when we were filthy. His love picks us up when we fall. Remember, we did nothing to "win Him over" to begin with. He pursued us! His love was so intense for us that He made a way for us to be together.

> But God - so rich is He in His mercy! Because of and *in order to satisfy the great and wonderful and intense love with which He loved us*, even when we were dead (slain) by (our own) shortcomings and trespasses, He made us alive together in fellowship and in union with Christ; (He gave us the very life of Christ Himself, the same new life with which He quickened Him, for) it is by grace (**His** favor and mercy which you did not deserve) that you are saved (delivered from judgment and made partakers of Christ's salvation).
>
> —Ephesians 2:4-5, AMP
> (emphasis added)

One day while spending time with God, I saw this picture in my mind: I was standing on the top of a trophy base. Rather than being metal, plastic, or wood, the foundation was made from the most beautiful glass I've ever seen. It was so pure that it looked "diamondy." There just aren't enough English words to describe how perfect and beautiful it was. I felt the Lord tell me that the mixture used to form the base had nothing mixed into it--it was unadulterated grace. He began to explain to me that, as His trophy, I was to stand on nothing other than His pure grace. He told me that NOTHING (works, religion, legalism, or striving) can be mixed into the base. What He provided for us to stand on is more perfect than anything else we can try to grab a hold of. We are not to try to mix anything into the foundation because His grace is more than sufficient —it's perfect.

You see, God never intended for us to leave our "B.C." (Before Christ) bondage of sin to simply exchange it for a "holier version" of bondage. **He wants a relationship and intimacy with us!** He gave up everything for a *"chance* to be with us." Do you know that there was no guarantee that Jesus' sacrifice would pay off in your life personally? In other words, each of us has a free will, and we can choose to accept Him or not. Imagine that. Even still, knowing that you could choose to reject Him, He suffered and died for the *chance* that He could be together with you! That's love. It's not the kind of love that requires you to *earn* it, or to even *maintain* it. Let's face it, the truth of the matter is our very best efforts are as filthy as dirty rags compared to His goodness and glory.

CHALLENGE

- Do you ever think that God just requires too much?
- Do you feel like you can't do anything right or that you are continually failing God?
- When you've tried your hardest, do you still feel like it's just not enough?
- Do you struggle with perfectionism?
- Do you feel close to God when you've made good decisions but far from Him when you've messed up?
- Do you understand the difference between conviction and condemnation?
- Do you run **to** the Father or run **from** the Father when you sin?
- Are you confident that your sins have been forgiven, or do you find yourself still carrying the guilt of them?
- When things don't go well, do you think God is punishing you?
- Are you enjoying your relationship with God? Or does it feel more like a burden?

- Do you believe you are righteous even when you
  don't do everything right?

I want to remind you of 2 Corinthians 5:21 which says, "For our sake He made Christ (virtually) to be sin Who knew no sin, so that in and through Him we might become (endued with, **viewed as being in,** and examples of) the righteousness of God (what we ought to be, approved and acceptable and in right relationship with Him, by His goodness)" (AMP).

God's criteria or His reason for loving us isn't based on what we do or don't do! Although I had experienced God's forgiveness and knew beyond a shadow of a doubt that my sins had been paid for, it took me years to realize that I couldn't be good enough to deserve it and didn't have to try to "**pay Him back.**" It was almost like I was trying to prove with my behavior that He didn't die in vain and I was worth the sacrifice.

So if you are living in a way that you're trying, knowingly or unknowingly, "to win Him over," you will be frustrated and disappointed. Why? Because we can never be good enough to be loved more than we are right now!

If you are in this vicious cycle, please allow the Holy Spirit to reveal the truth to you, heal you, and stop the cycle. Living like this steals your joy of walking with the One Who loves you beyond your wildest imagination!

PRAYER

God, You are my Father, and You paid the highest price for the opportunity to win my heart. **You** *came through Jesus because You loved me and wanted to save me. I know that I cannot add one thing to what You've already done, but I find myself not walking in the fullness of Your grace. Will You change that for me?*

By trying to be good enough for You to love me, I believed the lie that You love my good behavior more than You love me. Open my eyes to see how much You love me. I belong to You. You are the Author and the Finisher of my faith. I lay my efforts, work, and self-righteousness at Your feet. They will never be enough. I receive the free gift of forgiveness and righteousness that You paid for.

My hope is in **You**, *not in* **my** *efforts. I do not want to be pushed around by guilt, condemnation, or works any longer. I am Your beloved child, loved and forgiven. I don't want those to just be words that I say; I want to know that I know them. I want them to be my reality!*

I ask You to heal all the broken places in me. I want all the obstacles removed so I can intimately know Your passionate love and beautiful grace! Thank You, Papa, for loving me so much that YOU came through Jesus. Open my eyes to the truth that is found in Your Word. Amen.

7

THERE IS SOMETHING WRONG WITH ME
EXPOSING SHAME & REJECTION

*C*an I tell you what was even worse than the legalism and performance in my life? Rejection and shame! When I got my life reasonably "cleaned up" of the visible sins, things would still go wrong, and this lingering thought would pop up: *"See, your 'good' isn't even good enough for Him; therefore, the problem must be **you**."* After all, I was a *"highly functioning Christian,"* so if that wasn't enough, then clearly, **who I was** had to be the problem! No matter what I did, there was this constant and nagging sense that I was unacceptable.

Those were my lowest times. When all my efforts didn't seem to "earn" me God's favor, I assumed that I was simply unlovable! I was a disappointment to my earthly father, and deep in my heart I believed that I was a disappointment to my Heavenly Father. Sometimes I felt like a failure to almost everyone, even my husband and kids. I would compare myself to others that had been Christians all of their lives and assumed that the reason things "appeared" to be going so well for them must have been because God loved them more and they weren't tainted like I was.

Again, these thoughts and realizations were *not* at the forefront of my mind. They were more like hidden and quiet assumptions. They were secretly hiding in my soul, below all my "rational" thoughts but still affecting me in undetected ways. Even though the Bible was telling me the complete opposite, my soul wasn't receiving the truth. It was when I allowed the Holy Spirit to show me what I *really* thought and believed in my *soul*, that I realized the contradiction that existed. I was really living *through* those filters! In reality, I had been "building" upon a cracked foundation. No wonder the elaborate creation I had manufactured wasn't holding up.

Shame

In my opinion, shame is a crippling, emotional demon. However, *Vocabulary.com* says shame is a painful feeling that's a mix of regret, self-hate, and dishonor.[1] According to the Merriam-Webster dictionary, the definition of shame is a feeling of guilt, regret, or sadness that you have because you know you have done something wrong.[2] I would like to add, because you *think* you've done something wrong.

To me, shame is more profound than "knowing you've done something wrong." This disgusting enemy *doesn't care "if" you've done something wrong.* As a matter of fact, many times the person may not have even done anything wrong. Often, *something wrong* was done to them. Yes, I sensed regret over some things that I had done, but, for the most part, I experienced *more* shame over *who I was*.

My dad enjoyed making jokes at the expense of others. I honestly don't think he really knew the damage he was doing. I think he just didn't have any other communication skills so he resorted to that one painfully sharp tool that he knew so well. He would often humiliate me when we were around his drunk male friends. This carved deep scars on my young teenage heart. I was trying to figure out who I was, which is hard enough in and of itself. However, having the one man in your life who is supposed to adore you and think you're awesome be the one that is teasing and embarrassing you like a bully on the playground, is very painful. Common sense tried to tell my brain that he was just teasing, but the hatefulness and spitefulness behind his words told me otherwise.

Each of us wants to be unique and special. We want to be different enough to stand out to someone in a good way but not so different that others look at us as if there is something "wrong" with us. We were designed by a God that knitted us together uniquely and on purpose (Psalm 139:13). He then gives us to parents that are supposed to be the *first* example here on earth of what it means to be uniquely and unconditionally loved and adored. When children do not receive that, I think it etches an ugly message onto their souls. If the "acceptance foundation" isn't formed the way it's supposed to be, this can cause a deep-rooted feeling of shame and rejection. Without even realizing it we can start building on a "what's wrong with me" foundation instead of an "I am loved and accepted" foundation.

Shame has a way of making you believe you are dirty, ugly, and of no value. Shame tells you that you're different from everyone else. It holds you to a different standard. Any time I'd start to believe that I might be okay, shame had a way of yanking me right back to its side.

Rejection

Rejection is a very damaging cycle. What's sad about it is that you may not even realize that it's running your life **because you probably believe it is true!** For example, when the Holy Spirit would try to reveal the truth to me about myself, I would struggle to accept it because I was afraid to ignore

"*my*" reality. In other words, whenever I would try to receive
what God would say about me, I would talk myself out of it
because deep in my soul I believed that I was rejected, so I
lived rejected. I wasn't about to be soft on myself!

I not only felt forsaken and even jilted by God at times, but
rejection reared its disgusting head in so many other areas of
my life. If my husband or children, or anyone for that matter,
wasn't happy with me, I really took it to heart, but not in a
balanced way. In other words, it devastated me. For so long, if
I would receive any hint of disappointment from someone, it
felt like monumental rejection. When I would try to step back
and look at it with a more balanced look, I was too hard on
myself because I was afraid of not being hard enough on
myself. It's a crazy cycle.

I wanted my husband and my children to be open and honest,
but when they were, it would crush me. What may have been
something for me to consider or possibly change became such
a bigger and more painful issue. It really seemed more like a
personal rejection. I truly did want their honesty, but I just
didn't know how to separate my *actions* from my "*who*."

You see, shame and rejection weren't just something that
happened to me; they had become "who" I believed I was. So,
when God's word said I was chosen, accepted in the beloved,
forgiven, and righteous, I struggled to *really* believe that about
myself. I recognized that about everyone else, but I struggled
to take it for myself. It was easy to see God's grace for others,
regardless of their past, but for some reason, I struggled to
believe it applied to me. The truth is, I had even rejected
myself.

I unconsciously expected that my husband would eventually
get sick of me and leave me. Others had abandoned me, so I
expected him to do the same. No matter how well things were
going in our marriage, I would dream on a very regular basis

that he would cheat on me. Or, in the dream, he would finally tell me the truth that he wasn't happy with me all along and was leaving. This went on for way too many years.

Joyce Meyer has a teaching on *The Spirit of Rejection.* I listened to it very early on in my walk with Jesus, and it certainly helped. It is a powerful teaching. I recommend that everyone listen to it, even if you don't think you are dealing with this issue. Many years later, I listened to it again, but this time, it made so much more sense. I could clearly see how rejection was affecting me. As I started walking in that knowledge and truth, I saw some real changes occur in my life.

However, one evening, sometime after listening to those tapes, I woke up, startled from another, similar dream. Just as I opened my eyes, I saw something that appeared to be an evil spirit, kind of disappear right before my eyes. Before I could start to rationalize it away, there was this boldness that rose up inside of me. I realized that the enemy had been caught, and I wasn't going to put up with it any longer.

I'm not going to get into whether Christians can have demons, or whether they are oppressed or possessed. That rabbit trail is for another day. However, I'm simply going to say that the Word is clear that there are angels and demons. I know that God allowed me to catch a glimpse of the one that was trying to influence my dreams negatively. I needed to see that it was a *spirit* of rejection and not me. The realization that this demon had been harassing me for all those years infuriated me! It was then that I sensed a righteous indignation rise within me, and I took authority over that lying spirit of rejection.

The remarkable thing is that God has given you and me authority over all the principalities and powers, and I was appalled that this lying demon had been secretly harassing me for years! I believed it was me and that it was the *truth* when all along it was a demonic influence (See Ephesians 6:12).

And you know what? I've had only one dream like that since, and that was when I was writing this section of the book! How convenient? The cool thing is, when I woke up, it didn't affect me the way it used to. It just didn't have the power over me that it once had. It was kind of comical since it just so happened to be exactly when I was sharing what God had done.

Does that mean that I will never *feel* rejected again? Of course not. I don't think the enemy is going to give up that easily. Besides, against our best efforts, we will intentionally and unintentionally hurt one another. We all have plenty of opportunities to feel and be rejected. So, it is imperative that we KNOW God's love and acceptance fully for ourselves. However, what I've found since this soul belief has been exposed is that I'm walking in more victory than ever before. The more I realize how crazy God is about me, the stronger I become.

The Holy Spirit took me to an even deeper level of healing and deliverance in this area just a few years ago. Let me explain. During a time of worship, I was lying on the floor. All of the sudden, it was like I zoomed out, and I could see myself lying on the floor. I noticed that there were heavy shackles wrapped around my arms; however, they were not only unlocked, but also open. I immediately knew God was saying that He had already set me free, as the restraints were unlocked and open. However, the shackles were still too close to my arms, hindering me. As I watched this scenario play out before me, I saw myself stand up and get away from the iron handcuffs. I was watching myself jumping up and down in freedom when I heard Him say to me, "Turn around and look down." I expected to see the chains laying on the floor, but instead, I saw the chalk outline of my body! I heard Him say, "A death has occurred here. Now, live free of this!"

Without even realizing it, I had been allowing that rejection to hang out close to me. The shackles were open because Jesus had already set me free, but I found that I was being overly conscientious of my behavior again, questioning whether I was talking too much or not talking enough. I silently cared way too much what people thought of me. It made me afraid just to be who God created me to be. By God showing me the outline of myself and telling me that I had died myself, it freed me in a new way. You and I cannot fully walk in the freedom and power of God if we are bound or hindered in these ways. Uncovering the lies we believe is monumental.

When I say that I don't think the enemy will give up that easily, I'm saying that we have to walk in the revelation of the **truth** so we can identify his tactics and walk in freedom, regardless of what we think or feel. We cannot get into agreement with the enemy! The negative soul beliefs must be exposed before we can wholeheartedly *receive* the truth.

Paul said in 2 Corinthians 10:3-5: "For though we walk (live) in the flesh, we are not carrying on our warfare according to the flesh and using mere human weapons. For the weapons of our warfare are not physical (weapons of flesh and blood), but they are mighty before God **for the overthrow and destruction of strongholds**, (Inasmuch as we) refute arguments and theories and reasonings and every proud and lofty thing that sets itself up against the (true) knowledge of God; and we lead every thought and purpose away captive into the obedience of Christ (the Messiah, the Anointed One)…" (AMP).

We need to be able to identify when our thoughts do not line up with the Word of God so that we can "war" in the proper way. That requires exposing lies as well as stopping demonic activity. When you get into agreement with something nega-tive about yourself (and even others), you are labeling or passing a sentence on yourself (or them). Once you've labeled yourself and others, you give it validity because you believe what *you* think probably more than you believe anyone else! Jesus purchased you, so you are usurping what He says about **His** creation, the one He loves immensely.

We can all experience a "feeling" of being rejected by some-one, but I think there is a difference when you embrace it or when it really is what you think about yourself. The only way I can describe it is to say it's like an internal attack, rather than an outward one. The enemy wants you and I to feel rejected, because when we feel rejected, we tend to withdraw. When we disengage from people, we lose intimacy. He also wants us to feel rejected so we will hold back and not whole-heartedly walk in all that God has for us! We will miss out on so much that God has for us if we allow rejection or shame to control our lives.

And most of all, the devil wants you to feel rejected so you won't realize that you are greatly loved. God's love for YOU is beyond your imagination. Ephesians 3:18-19 (AMP) says: "That you may have the power and be strong to apprehend and grasp with all the saints (God's devoted people, the *experi-ence* of that love) what is the breadth and length and height and depth (That you may really come) to know (practically, **through *experience* for yourselves**) the love of Christ, which far surpasses mere knowledge (*without experience*); that you may be filled (through all your being) unto all the fullness of God (may have the measure of the divine Presence, and become a body wholly filled and flooded with God Himself)!" (AMP). Look at that! He wants us to *experience* His love and not just have *head knowledge* that He loves us. When that happens, it's like everything in the Word drops from your head into your heart, and you are transformed. For way too many years, I only "experienced" His love through faith and sheer determination, but God wants each of us to experience the real deal!

Some might say, "You just have to remind yourself and the enemy **Whose** you are and how much God loves you!" That's so true. Although, the only problem is, if those are just words on a paper to you, it won't help much. When I didn't understand my right-standing with God and was still trying to acquire it, I would read a scripture that said something like, "For those who are righteous, I will…" and I would *unconsciously* exclude myself in that promise because I couldn't believe that I was righteous in God's eyes. Instead, I would think that maybe that promise **could** be for me but only if I could be good enough. It's so deceitful. We can never be good enough to earn what God has done for us. Did I say that already? Yes, I did! I just can't say it enough!

Therefore, we must allow the Holy Spirit to reveal any negative soul beliefs, or wounds, in our lives and let Him heal us so that we can enjoy the *intimate* love of our Father. He wants the truths in the Bible to *become* truth to us! Only when the lies are exposed can God begin to debunk them. If I had never realized that I viewed Him in these ways, then I wouldn't have been able to experience breakthrough. I would have kept reading the Word without seeing the fruit of truly **believing** the Word.

CHALLENGE

Rejection and shame are two things that most of us deal with at one time or another. They can enter our lives in the most tragic of circumstances or in the most innocent of ways. It can come from a parent who intentionally or unintentionally compared you to a sibling or made you feel like you could never do anything right. It can happen in the classroom, on the playground, at your workplace, and pretty much anywhere else. It can arise from an incident involving those that are supposed to love you the most and even from a stranger. It often occurs in divorce.

- Do you struggle with feeling unacceptable, unlovable, dirty, or unworthy?
- Do you struggle with comparison?
- Do you have a hard time believing that you are greatly loved?
- Do you find yourself thinking people are mad at you?
- Do you ever think that you're seriously flawed or that there's just something not right with you?

- Do you struggle to be real with others, afraid that they will reject you if they knew the real you?
- Do you have a hard time feeling like you fit in or belong?
- Is it difficult to receive constructive criticism?
- Are you having a hard time forgiving yourself or others?
- Do you find yourself trying to be what you think others think you should be?
- Do you struggle with trying to please others and then get upset because you just can't seem to please them?
- Do you say no to opportunities out of fear that you'll be rejected?
- Do you struggle with feeling dirty or sinful even though you have asked God to forgive you?
- Do you feel like God or others disapprove of you?
- Do you ever feel that God is just tolerating you?

I have wonderful news for you! Shame and rejection were placed upon Jesus and crucified on the cross! They have been defeated! Exposing the lies that cause shame and rejection and putting them on the cross, brings freedom.

Isaiah 53:3-4 tells us about Jesus...

> He was despised and **rejected** and forsaken by men, a Man of sorrows and pains, and acquainted with grief and sickness; and like One from Whom men hide their faces He was despised, and we did not appreciate His worth or have any esteem for Him. Surely He has borne our griefs (sicknesses, weaknesses, and distresses) and carried our sorrows and pains (of punishment) yet we (ignorantly) considered Him stricken, smitten, and afflicted by God (as if with leprosy). (AMP)

Our beautiful Jesus was perfect, and yet, He was hung naked on a sinner's cross to take our place. He not only suffered physical pain from the scourging and the nails, but He suffered rejection and humiliation. He knows what you have been through. He knows what it feels like to be falsely accused and "done wrong." He was acquainted with grief, sorrow, and pain, and He did that for you! You can give Him your pain, shame, sadness, and rejection. He is not afraid of it. Keeping it hidden in your soul is not the way to get free. Instead, give it to Him because He was acquainted with it and defeated it.

God didn't get stuck with you! It wasn't like He just "inherited" you because of what Jesus did. No, God actually finds pleasure in you because He designed and created you. He accepts you, not because He must, but because He wants to! The Father not only loves you, but He sincerely likes you.

PRAYER

God, Your love for me is exceptionally greater than I can possibly imagine. You paid the highest of prices in hopes of having a relationship with me. You have not ever rejected me, and You never will! I desire to have an intimate relationship with You and others. I don't want works, performance, rejection, or shame to interfere with me experiencing the fullness of Your love.

Thank You for defeating rejection and shame on the cross. I give them to You so that You can make something beautiful out of them. They have no power over me! I am free from rejection because of Your blood, in Jesus' name.

When circumstances and the enemy try to make me believe anything but the truth, I ask You to help me to catch it right away and to stand against it. Help me to hide the Truth in my heart and not just my head. Only You can make this truth to me.

Thank You for healing me and setting me free so that I can receive and give love. I am fully accepted by You! Make that so real to me, in the name of Jesus, I pray. Amen.

8

THE BEAUTIFUL JOURNEY
FROM ORPHAN TO BELOVED

*B*eing in the Father's love and presence produced more fruit and changes in my life than striving and working for years had ever done! Because God is so good, it didn't take long before my precious Father began to show me even more. One day, while I was just spending time in God's presence, I saw a few scenes from the movie *Annie* flash across my mind. For anyone who might not be aware of it, *Annie* is a story about a little girl who is being raised in an orphanage by the mean Miss Hannigan. She's lived a "hard knock" life but is later adopted by a very wealthy man named, "Daddy Warbucks."

I asked God why that movie flashed in my mind. He said that even though I had discovered His goodness, I was still living like an orphan. I had finally perceived and believed that God was good, and He didn't cause bad things to happen to people. Now, He was showing me that I had a different filter that I was living from, one of an orphan.

If you've ever seen the movie, you'll know what I'm talking about. The children in the orphanage were being "super-vised" by Miss Hannigan, a woman who didn't care about the children at all. As a matter of fact, they were more of a burden and a nuisance to her.

Annie and the other orphans did not receive love. They barely received the most basic of provisions but only if they did everything right and completed their chores. The caretaker was not interested in the children, just in what they could do for **her**. Sound familiar? That's how I had viewed God.

As I talked to the Father about what He was showing me, I realized that I was still operating and thinking like an orphan, not a beloved daughter. It was a subtle thought process, but a detrimental one. He began to show me how the children from *Annie* might have felt and the way they behaved. Let's look at it.

An orphan is used to working and earning so that they may be taken care of. When Annie was brought to the house that would eventually become her new home, she automatically assumed that she was there to serve with the hired help. As an orphan, she always had to earn her keep. She couldn't believe that someone would want her for something other than what she could do for them!

Orphans can grow accustomed to doing without. While at the orphanage, Annie received the bare minimum, but she could easily and quickly lose that, too. If she didn't behave, she could be punished by having her necessities withheld. Orphans **hope** to be taken care of, but they don't always expect it, and they certainly don't anticipate extravagance.

Annie and the other orphans had to take care of themselves. Miss Hannigan was self-absorbed, uncaring, and even abusive. She did not have their best interests at heart. They ultimately knew they were responsible for themselves. Many had lost their childhood and were forced to grow up too quickly. Those children didn't get to experience the unearned, carefree provision and protection of a loving parent.

Miss Hannigan didn't provide love or acceptance, either. These orphans didn't know what it was like to be loved or adored. They were rejected, not only by their parents, but by the one who was supposed to be providing a home for them. Of course, not all parents had rejected them. Some may have died, which of course was no fault of their own. However, death can still *feel* like rejection. Orphans can grow to expect rejection, so they automatically exclude themselves because withdrawing is easier to deal with than being rejected.

Orphans tend to plan for the worst and anticipate broken promises. They've learned that it's better not to expect than to be disappointed. Maybe they hoped and dreamed for years to be loved enough for someone to want them, only to be rejected year after year. Even if they do get "adopted," they often wait for things to go wrong. In other words, they can generally live with a low level of expectancy.

Life tends to be "serious" for orphans. They typically can't fathom what it's like to be carefree. They are forced into the "real world" reality way too soon. This can really affect their ability to enjoy life and people. Life tends to feel heavy and burdensome to them. They can be more acquainted with work and struggle than rest, freedom, and joy.

You don't have to be an actual orphan to think and behave like one. As a matter of fact, I think Christians often live like orphans without even being aware of it. Many of us don't expect God's attention, provision, protection, approval, or love.

We've talked so much in previous chapters about knowing God for who He really is. For me, I had finally started to get to know the real Father God. I had wrestled with the negative beliefs that I had of the Father and my life did change significantly. However, He was now showing me that we needed to address my orphan tendencies.

Very early in my walk with God, I received a prophetic word from a prophet/pastor that came to our church. In the middle of the prophecy, he said, "God is not dealing with you as an orphan, but as a daughter." I wish I could say those words changed everything for me. Sadly, it took many more years for me to realize that I sometimes viewed God as an orphanage caretaker.

I had been trained by the way I grew up to not hope for much. I knew how to be content with very little. I was like Annie; the necessities were enough for me. I certainly didn't want to "push my luck" and ask for more. However, the more I discovered about God, the more I wanted! There were some things that I had been praying about for a long time, things that I knew were in God's will. After a couple of years, I really started getting frustrated. That's when God played the *Annie* scene for me.

Remember when I mentioned that Annie walked into Mr. Warbucks' house and immediately assumed she was there as part of the hired help? She did not realize that she was there because he was taking her as his daughter! Well, that is what myself and many others have done in the church. We hear about this God that wants to welcome us into His family, and we accept. We walk into the church with our servant/orphan mindsets and start "working" like the hired help.

Because I did not know how to **be** a beloved daughter, I had the unspoken, unrealized attitude that I was working *for* Jesus, not partnering *with* Jesus. I acted like an orphan that had to earn her keep instead of a daughter who was incredibly loved and accepted, regardless of what I did or didn't do. Trust me, I'm not putting down servanthood, but it should be done out of the abundance of our relationship with God, not as a means of trying to get a relationship with Him. I heard Kris Vallotton say *something* like this: If we teach new believers how to be workers before they know they are sons (or daughters), we create workers or slaves.

Just as Oliver Warbucks chose Annie to be his daughter and not the hired help, God wants us to be His sons and daughters, not His hired helpers. Just like Annie's new father, God doesn't "need" us to be His workers, enslaved, trying to earn our keep. I repeat, when we are adopted, we become God's sons and daughters, not part of the hired help.

Serving others is a joyous privilege, but it doesn't feel like it if your motivation is skewed. I honestly had a heart of compassion, and I genuinely wanted to help others, but my heart was *contaminated* with an orphan mentality which stood in my way of learning to just "be" His beloved daughter.

Jack Frost said this:

> *"Often within the church, it is difficult to tell whether a person walks in the heart attitude of an orphan or a son (this includes daughters). Outwardly, a person may have a pattern of service, sacrifice, discipline and apparent loyalty, but you do not know what is inside a person until he or she gets bumped. Then the attitude of the heart overflows at a time when they feel they are not getting the recognition or favor they deserve."*[1]

There is such a difference when you know that you are emphatically loved just for who you are and not for what you do. Am I saying that new believers shouldn't serve? No, but as individuals, we need to examine our motives and attitudes "when we get bumped." Are we helping others out of a source of joy, or is it for some other reason? Likewise, as leaders, we need to make sure we are teaching the grace-filled, Father

Heart of God, because I think we'd all be shocked if we could see how many people struggle with this.

Another problem with having an orphan "filter" is that we will not be aware of our real identity. Rather than living victorious, we will struggle to just get by. No wonder the enemy wants us to live like orphans. He doesn't want us to realize that we are sons and daughters of **THE KING**. Truthfully, we hand Him our filthy rags, and He puts a crown on our heads. You don't typically see a prince or princess living like a pauper. They know who they are, and they know the authority and power that has been given to them. No doubt, Satan never wants us to realize that we are heirs of the King!

Here are just a few scriptures on adoption:

> Yet all of this was so that he would redeem and set free all those held hostage to the written law so that we would receive our freedom and a full legal adoption as his children.
>
> —Galatians 4:5, TPT

> And you did not receive the "spirit of religious duty," leading you back into the fear of never being good enough. But you have received the "Spirit of Full Acceptance," enfolding you into the family of God. And you will never feel orphaned, for as he rises up within us, our spirits join him in saying the words of tender affection, "Beloved Father!" For the Holy Spirit makes God's fatherhood real to us as he whispers into our innermost being, "You are God's beloved child!" And since we are his true children, we qualify to share all his treasures, for indeed, we are heirs of God himself. And since we are joined to Christ, we also inherit all that he is and all that he has. We will experience being co-glorified

with him provided that we accept his sufferings as
our own.

—Romans 8:15, TPT

For it was always in his perfect plan to adopt us as his
delightful children, through our union with Jesus, the
Anointed One, so that his tremendous love that cascades
over us would glorify his grace-for the same love he has for
his Beloved One, Jesus, he has for us. And this unfolding
plan brings him great pleasure!

—Ephesians 1:5-6, TPT

New Birth Certificate

According to adopt.org, when a child is adopted, an amended
birth certificate is issued. Check this out: An **amended birth
certificate** is:

a birth certificate issued after a child has been adopted.
It's like the original birth certificate, but instead, it
names the adoptive parents as the parents. An adopted
child will have both an adoption certificate and a birth
certificate, *although* **he or she may have access
only to the amended on**[2]

I love that. It says, "... *he or she may have access only to
the amended one.*"[3] That is awesome. That's how perma-
nent the adoption is! So, the adoption legally changed Annie's
name as if she had **always** been a "Warbucks," and she no
longer was identified by her previous name!

Well, that is what God does when He adopts us. First, we should realize that it is God who initiated the adoption. Ephesians 1:5 says that in **love** He predestined us for adoption to sonship through Jesus Christ. It was always God's plan to make us His own!

Oliver "Daddy" Warbucks knew that Annie was a poor orphan and that she had *nothing* to offer him. **He** was the one who had it all! He was the wealthy, powerful and influential one. The only thing she had to offer was herself--her love. What a beautiful picture of what God does for us.

As impressive as that was for Annie, our adopted Father's love puts Daddy Warbucks' love to shame. Our Papa's love is so committed that He gave up His one and only Son for all of us orphans to become His beloved children. His love is unadulterated and perfect. Ephesians 1:5 says that God has the same love for **us** as He does for his Beloved One, Jesus! What? Yes! God loves us as much as He loves His sinless Son, Jesus! That is mind blowing.

Our incredibly good and loving Father does not want us to live like servants nor orphans. His sacrifice was enormous, and it was for the very purpose of becoming our Father, not our taskmaster. He doesn't want us to try to work for "our keep." He doesn't want us to try to earn His favor. He doesn't want us to expect broken promises, rejection, or disappointment. When we have that type of mindset, it affects how we live and relate to Him. It will also change how we relate to others.

If we think or feel like orphans, we will *live* like orphans. Proverbs 23:7 says, "As he [a person] thinks in his heart, so is he" (AMP).

The King, our Father, has bequeathed or bestowed upon us all these things, but if we don't realize who we are, we won't walk in them or even expect them. 2 Peter 1:3 says, "Everything we could ever need for life and complete devotion to God has already been deposited in us by his divine power. *For all this was lavished upon us* through the rich experience of knowing him who has called us by name and invited us to come to him through a glorious manifestation of his goodness" (TPT).

He's provided it for us, but if we don't think it's ours, because we view ourselves as orphans, we won't receive it. In other words, all that is ours will be abandoned or forfeited.

Our birth certificates have been amended! We are to no longer have access to the original one. We should **not** live according to our "original birth certificate"—the one that says wretched sinner, loser, slave, etc.—but instead live according to the one that proves we are sons and daughters of the Most High. Our Father is the King, and we are His beloved children. We are co-heirs with Christ. His name is listed on our birth certificate!

God could have saved us and taken us in as hired help, but He didn't. He wanted us to be His children instead. For those of us that didn't have the best example of a father or parent, that can be a challenge, but not an impossibility. I am entirely convinced that He wants to reveal His Father-heart to each of us. For that to happen, we must be willing to let go of the preconceived and religious ideas and allow the Spirit of Truth to reveal who the Father really is. In verse 16, the Apostle Peter continued, saying, "For the Holy Spirit makes God's fatherhood real to us and He whispers into our innermost being, 'You are God's beloved child!'" (2 Peter 1:16, TPT).

Do I still find myself dealing with orphan tendencies? Yep, they still pop up, but I'm a beautiful work in progress. Besides, the enemy is determined, so he will not stop trying to launch fiery darts at any of us. He's hoping that at least one will penetrate and that I will get into agreement with him. Truthfully, do I have an orphaned heart? NO! I do *not* have an orphaned heart.

Think about that, God would never "orphan" our hearts, as that would make Him a terrible father. Besides, it is completely opposite to the Word of God. The enemy would like to make you and I believe otherwise. He'd like to put glasses on us that would cause us to see things like an orphan would. Satan wants us to have orphan thoughts because it will keep us from our destiny, and his goal is to keep us from the Heart of the Father. What better way to do that than to make us feel like orphans or slaves? A slave absolutely isn't going to call his master Daddy.

When Jesus departed this earth, He didn't leave us as orphans (John 14:16-18). He left us the Holy Spirit, the Spirit of Truth. So, when my Father saw that I had a soul belief that was contrary to the truth, He spoke to me through that movie. You see, Papa knows everything that you and I have been through. He's not mad at us. Our Daddy LOVES us! So, when I have wrong thinking, He is faithful and happy to reveal the truth to me. He doesn't say, "Tammy, how much longer is it going to take before you get this? I've already done it all for you, but you're still dealing with this?" No, He didn't talk to me like that. He lovingly reveals the truth to us because He is the best Father!

Maybe you are like me, and you haven't yet fully realized the gravity and importance of Paul's use of the word *adoption*. After all, to be adopted you must have been orphaned, right? No one wants to be an orphan. For some, despite its beauty, the word *adoption* can have an underlying negative connotation because it reveals an initial loss. So, why would the Apostle Paul use adoption to describe what God does for us through Jesus when James and Peter refer to us as sons (daughters)? Does it even matter, especially if most people think that birth is the most ideal condition? Well, this is where knowing about their culture and laws makes a big difference.

For us to really understand the importance of Paul's word choice, we need to understand the **value** of the word <u>adopted</u> *during that specific time*, thus giving us a better picture of what God was telling us.

Adoption was a serious and deliberate matter in their culture. As a matter of fact, there were laws concerning it. Paul, even though he was Jewish, was a Roman citizen, and he knew the law. The Roman-Syrian Law Book indicated that, while the biological son could be disowned (with good reason), the *adopted* son could not be disowned! The one adopted had more protection and rights than the one with birthrights.[4]

Also, by looking at the writer's culture and laws, we see an even more glorious picture--an even more meaningful message. Paul takes God's role as Father even further and refers to us as being adopted because it promised more than just becoming part of God's family. This is because, according to Roman Law, the person being adopted would virtually appear to have never existed! Their name would not only change, but **all** debts would have been canceled. They literally got a new start.[5]

So, you can see how this would have had significant meaning to the people of that time. While the word <u>sons</u> would have resonated with the Jewish people, the Roman and even the Greek would have been equally moved by Paul's use of the word *adopted*.

When we look at God's adoption of us in the light of this knowledge, it means so much more! He is declaring, "You're not only my sons and daughters, which has great benefits, but I will never disown you! He's also saying, "I'm literally giving you a new life." In addition, if all that wasn't enough, He goes even further and seals the deal.

Adoptions back then would have required seven witnesses. This granted protection in case the adopter died and someone tried to deny the adoptee's inheritance. The witnesses would attest that the person had indeed been adopted and therefore able to access what was rightfully theirs.[6] Well, I have good news. We have a witness to our adoption, too!

> The Spirit Himself bears witness with our spirit that we are children of God,
>
> —Romans 8:16, NKJV

> For the Holy Spirit makes God's fatherhood real to us as he whispers into our innermost being, "You are God's beloved child!"
>
> —Romans 8:16, TPT

> The Spirit Himself (thus) testifies together with our own spirit, (assuring us) that we are (His) heirs also; heirs of God and fellow heirs with Christ (sharing His inheritance with Him);
>
> —Romans 8:16, AMP

CHALLENGE

As I mentioned before, you don't have to experience being an actual orphan or servant to have an orphan mentality. Any experience of abandonment, rejection, or disappointment can open the door to this stronghold. Here are some questions for you to ask yourself to see if you are thinking or perceiving in any way other than as a beloved son or daughter:

- Do you have a hard time trusting people and/or God?
- Do you feel misunderstood, unloved, or lonely most of the time?
- Do you feel like you must take care of yourself because "no one else will"?
- Do you worry you'll not have enough? Do you hold onto things out of fear?
- Do you get jealous when you see others blessed or feel threatened by others' success?
- Do you find yourself trying to outdo others?

- Do you secretly take satisfaction in the weaknesses of others?
- Do you find your identity in what you do, what you look like, or what you have?
- Do you find yourself needing the affirmation of others?
- Are you defensive when corrected? Do you always feel the need to be right?
- Are you easily offended?
- Are you struggling with insecurity or low self-esteem?
- Do you tend to criticize and complain?
- Do you volunteer but then find yourself complaining about it?
- Do you struggle with authority?
- Do you often feel overlooked or unappreciated?
- Do you have a hard time getting along with people?
- Do you tend to be a lone ranger?
- Do you expect to be disappointed? Are you afraid to hope for more?
- Do you know how to rest and have fun or is that a struggle for you?

You know, it doesn't surprise me that Satan tries so hard to attack us with these types of thoughts and this way of thinking. After all, the very heart of God the Father is to adopt us, to make us His own! Satan realizes that if we discover and walk in our true identity, it will change everything.

Can you just imagine if all of God's children understood how incredibly loved they are? We would rejoice when others are promoted and recognized because we would be confident in God's love for us! We would not be jealous because we would be assured that God has something different for us. We would not have to struggle to make things happen, but instead, we would live in peace, knowing our good Father has it all under control. Our service would be from a place of joy. When we are confident in God's individual love for us, we don't feel the need to drag others down to make us feel better. Competition becomes camaraderie.

When we are convinced of who and whose we are, it frees us to be who we really are. It's when we are trying to be something we are not that we behave like someone we are not.

PRAYER

Oh Father, thank You for adopting me. I am no longer an orphan, so I don't want to live like one! You hand-picked me to be Yours. My new birth certificate says I am Yours, a child of THE KING. Your adoption of me is final, and I have access only to my new birth certificate.

I realize that some areas of my life still need healing. I want to live the life You paid for. I repent for believing the lies. I renounce the orphan spirit, and I break its power over my life. I declare that I am a treasured child of the perfect Father, God.

I ask You to change the way that I think, perceive, and act. Teach me how to rest in Your love. I want to receive the love You've poured out for me. I want to be so confident in Your love for me. I want to be unwaveringly convinced about my place in Your heart so that I do not have to struggle or work to be loved. I want to enjoy my relationship with You.

I'm tired of trying to get my identity from works, things, achievements or acknowledgments. Open my eyes to see how much You love and value me, not for what I do, but just for being me. Whisper into my innermost being so I KNOW that I am Your beloved child!

9

SCAR TISSUE
THE ENEMY'S PLAN

*U*ncovering the negative soul beliefs and allowing God to heal me produced more change in my life than anything else I had ever experienced before. His presence was changing me. I truly began to enjoy my relationship with Him. My intimacy with God went to new levels. Having my foundation healthy helped me so much when challenges came.

So, does that mean that once you've dealt with a soul belief that you'll never have to deal with it again? Oh, how I wish that were true, but it's not. Unfortunately, the devil plays for keeps. He will do anything he can to try to convince you and me to **give back territory**.

Several years after discovering the goodness of the Father and experiencing *years* of freedom from fear, the enemy tried to pry open that door again. In doing so, though, he unintentionally let his secret plan be exposed. Let me explain.

My husband and I were playing racquetball, as we did almost daily. We had already played four games, but because he had beaten me at all of them, I wanted another chance (No, I'm not competitive!). As I turned to run toward the ball to return it, my sneaker decided not to go with me. It happened so quickly and unexpectedly that I fell full force on my shoulder. I not only dislocated it, but I tore my tendon in two different places.

If you're not into health or science, I ask you to bear with me. I will try not to be too technical, but I really believe this is a great way to explain what the enemy tries to do when we are injured, betrayed, and even disappointed.

Physical Scar Tissue

Most of us have seen a scar on the outside of someone's body or even our own. However, did you know that you can develop scar tissue *inside* your body, where it is not visible? Scars are a natural part of the body's healing process. According to verywellhealth.com, "Scar tissue grows in the body as a normal response to injury."[1] It is your body's way of trying to protect and heal itself. To simplify it, the collagen cells that are meant to help you heal, end up clumping up and piling on top of each other, creating scar tissue.[2]

The team at the hospital had a difficult time trying to get my arm back into place, so I had to be knocked out for them to get my shoulder where it was supposed to be. I was put into a sling and unable to use my arm. My body quickly went into action to try to "protect and heal" itself. It started sending collagen fibers to that area to try to mend the damage. The result of all those "helpful" fibers, though, is that scar tissue was formed in my shoulder joint and all the surrounding injured areas. Again, from Verywellhealth.com, "While scar tissue is meant to be healthy, too much formation of a scar can cause problems."[3] So, by the time I was cleared for physical therapy, I had virtually no use of my right arm. When the therapist tested my range of motion, she pronounced that I had a "frozen shoulder."

I just assumed that physical therapy was going to be about simply re-strengthening my arm after not using it for so long. Oh boy, was I wrong. While that was true in part, *the key to the therapy was breaking up the scar tissue!* If that doesn't sound painful and difficult to you, let me assure you, it is. The mission was to gradually release the adhesions that had formed in the shoulder joint and surrounding wounded areas by using various painful techniques. I'm pretty tough, and I have a fairly high pain tolerance, but there were many days that I had to push through with tears rolling down my face. It was more than a seven-month painful battle to pry, stretch, pull, release, and otherwise, "remodel" the scar tissue in order to get my arm free.

The crazy thing was that from the moment that I was injured, something started happening to me. I could hear the enemy **screaming** at me, saying, "If *He* didn't protect you from this, you can't trust Him to protect your kids or your husband." I quickly recognized that old, familiar, accusing voice, and I stood against it! However, he was relentless. The battle was intense. I think he figured, "Let's go hard after her right now while she's hurt, confused, disappointed, weak, and injured."

To add insult to injury, this all happened during a season in my life when I was already going through *significant* challenges. I'll be honest. It was an all-out-fight to not buy into his lies. He was loud, and what he was saying sounded true. However, every time I'd hear an accusation, I'd stand against it. Even though I **felt** fear, I would say, "You are a liar, and I'm not going to get into agreement with you."

Every morning when I woke up, I was *immediately* faced with Satan's accusations. Day after day, I would do everything I knew to do to stand against them, but I wasn't seeing the breakthrough. If I heard a loud noise from one of my kids bounding down the stairs, I'd tense up, waiting for someone to start crying from an injury. When my husband would leave for work, I'd be struck with the fear that he would be in an accident. While I *refused to get into agreement* with the enemy, the battle kept raging! I was so frustrated by this because I had been living free from that type of fear for years. I had already dealt with that soul belief, so I couldn't understand how in the world I could "lose" my freedom.

One morning after months of battling this, I frustratingly said to my husband, "I am so sick of this! I can't hear God's voice over the devil's persistent threats. Between tears, I mumbled out something like, "I can't get him to shut up. It's almost like he's so close that I can feel him breathing on my face!" And that's when it happened. God broke through.

Suddenly, God revealed to me what was happening. As the words came tumbling out of my mouth, it was like a mental video started playing in my mind. I could see the devil, and he was hurling these accusations and lies at me just hoping that at least *one* would get through. There I was—injured, vulnerable, and incapacitated by my injury. I was trying to hold up the "shield of faith," but it seemed so *heavy*. And, if I'm honest, it didn't seem to be helping much, either. I wasn't just weary spiritually from the nonstop threats, I was exhausted in the natural from not being able to sleep for months from the pain and from having my arm in the sling. As the scene continued to unfold, I could see the father of lies was trying to move in close to me, and that's when I saw that he had a knife in his hand.

Suddenly, I knew what he was trying to do. His plan was to try to get me into agreement with the lies he was firing at me so he would get close enough to **carve them on my soul**! He was trying to use my painful and vulnerable condition as an opportunity to create another soul belief. He wanted to chisel them on my heart so they would form spiritual scar tissue!

Suddenly, everything made sense. I'd already been set free in this area, but the enemy wanted to try to put me back in prison. He wanted to try to convince me that I hadn't changed. He wanted my soul to believe again that I wasn't safe with God so I'd open the door wide and let fear move back in. In the same way that my shoulder had developed adhesions that were binding my arm, the enemy was trying to bind me with fear so I would be rendered "frozen." And, that is his goal for you, too.

Spiritual Scar Tissue

Satan is afraid of you, and he doesn't want you to walk in the freedom that Jesus gave you. He is determined to take every opportunity to try to put you and I in bondage. Then, on that day, God exposed **how** the enemy of our soul tries to go about creating these negative soul beliefs.

As Satan's goal is to steal, kill, and destroy you, he loves to make his move when you are wounded, betrayed, rejected, and vulnerable. When you've been hurt, the liar takes aim at your heart. He fires one arrow after another:

"You'll never be loved."

"You can't trust *anyone*."

"You're never going to be free."

"You should be ashamed of yourself."

"This is all your fault."

"You can't trust God."

"You're worthless."

On and on, he goes. *If* he can get you *into agreement with his lies,* he can move in even closer. This is when he takes his chisel and begins to carve "his" messages on your heart. You see, the enemy isn't *only* trying to get you to believe his lies, he wants to try to **engrave** them on your soul. He knows that if he is successful at etching them on the emotional part of you, they can create scar tissue that ultimately binds you or restricts you to some degree or another.

Have you ever noticed that when you walk near someone that has an injured leg, they will often quickly pull it closer into their body so you don't accidentally bump and further hurt them? That might seem completely normal at first. However, if they continue to do that for years *after* their leg has been healed, we'd wonder what was wrong with them. I think we do the same thing without realizing it. When we experience a traumatic event, are betrayed by someone we trusted, or we are repeatedly disappointed, it might not surprise us that we are out of commission for a little while. However, if we simply stuff it because we just want to move on, or if we deny it and don't allow God to rewrite the deceitful messages, scar tissue can form on our souls. The next thing you know, we are unintentionally "pulling back" our hearts, trying to avoid being further injured. It's not like we plan on "never loving again." We never wanted betrayal to cause us to stop trusting *everyone*, just the person who hurt us. These are unintentional responses to the pain we've experienced. It's us, unknowingly, trying to protect ourselves from something that can potentially harm us. This creates the perfect environment for adhesions to form.

The problem is that these kinds of responses are often unnoticed by us. After all, we have copious "reasons" for why we respond or act the way we do. We often justify our choices and behaviors. Many times, we're simply not aware that we are believing lies, holding back, or putting up walls. Therefore, negative soul beliefs are often left undetected. It takes the revelation of the Holy Spirit, our Great Physician, to reveal the damaging scars or lies that we are unknowingly believing.

Negative soul beliefs are like the unseen internal scars that can exist in our bodies. Neither are visible to the naked eye, but simply "not seeing them" doesn't mean they aren't affecting us. Both can wreak havoc if left untreated. Again, from Clearpassage.com, "Acting like powerful straitjackets, **adhesions** can squeeze nerves, organs and joints – causing internal pain or dysfunction including female fertility and life-threatening bowel obstructions."[4] They can even cause our *body's tissues and organs to adhere to one another* causing more damage.[5]

Well, spiritual adhesions can do the same thing. These messages can cause "spiritual infertility." They can form blockages that limit our intimacy and breakthrough. And, just like adhesions that can "attach" to other tissues and organs, negative soul beliefs can spread. They often lead to even more damaging soul beliefs. They certainly limit or hinder our freedom. They hold us back from loving whole-heartedly. They make us doubt God's love. They prevent us from doing what we are meant to do, and, most dangerously of all, they can unknowingly hinder us from believing God's Word.

Moving Forward: How to Protect Yourself

Ideally, we want to prevent the scars in the first place, but most of our soul beliefs were formed without us even realizing what was happening. You probably weren't aware that scar tissue was being weaved onto your heart when you suffered rejection, were cheated on, abused, or abandoned. I certainly didn't know those damaging messages were being imprinted on my little heart. I also wasn't aware that, through the years, those lies were being reinforced by new injuries. One gash after another, my heart was left bleeding and infected. Unknowingly, you and I can be open slates to write on.

However, once I met the beautiful Savior, He went to work, applying His healing balm to the different areas of my life. Through the years, I grew stronger and healthier, but sadly, until my "showdown" with God, I didn't realize that I still had some undetected *silent* scars left on my heart. Even as a sold-out, mature believer in Jesus, those sneaky little messages were still affecting me.

That's why we spent much of the previous chapters *uncovering* some common, negative soul beliefs. If we don't know they exist, we certainly won't deal with them. I hope that you have spent time in His presence allowing Him to uncover any negative soul beliefs. Now that we know they can exist and how they are formed, we can arm ourselves with the tools to prevent these lies from unknowingly being carved onto our souls. Knowing the enemy's scheme allows us to be on the offense, rather than the defense. It gives us a plan on how to protect ourselves when the liar tries to approach us with his carving tools in hand.

We know the enemy's intent is to render you "bound" in *any* area of your life so you will not be able to live, move, or have your being in Christ (Acts 17:28). I wish I could tell you that, as a believer in Jesus, you can avoid all pain and injury, but that's simply not true. Intentionally or unintentionally, even those that love us the most can hurt us. (If we're honest, we've hurt others as well.) Of course, we already know from John 10:10 that we have an enemy. Thankfully, Jesus said in John 16:33, "I have told you these things, so that in me you may have peace. In this world you will have trouble. But take heart! I have overcome the world" (TPT).

Earlier, when I told you about the mental video, I didn't tell you the rest of what I saw. The next scene looked like a Kung Fu fight right out of the movies. As the devil approached with a blade in his hand, I saw **myself** quoting scriptures. Hiyah! I blocked his arm. Every time I held up the shield of faith and feebly reminded myself that God was for me and not against me, it was like I was lifting up my arms in Bruce Lee style, WAHHHH! As I reminded the enemy of what God had already done for me, I karate chopped the knife right out of enemy's approaching hand.

Trust me, the entire time I was in the battle with fear, I never **felt** like a skilled, champion fighter. I was thoroughly disappointed to be fighting my old enemy again—the one I thought I had defeated once and for all. I was tired, in pain, and fearful. The battle up till then had been real and intense, and I didn't feel like I was winning. However, in the spirit realm, God was showing me that my seemingly weak efforts to stand on God's promises had actually been *preventing* the liar from writing his lies on my soul.

Once God showed me what was going on, I felt empowered and determined. I found myself facing a similar decision to the one that involved my shoulder. In order to get back the full use of my arm, I had to do the long and painful work required in physical therapy. If I would have tried to avoid the pain of trying to break down the connective tissue and would have refused to do the exercises involved, I would never have gained back the full use of my arm. Of course, I didn't **want** to continue to fight for my arm's freedom. It was painful, but the alternative was to accept the limitations of my arm and stay right where I was. I would never have been able to lift my grandchildren up in the air, fully hug anyone, or simply blow dry my own hair. Because I didn't want my arm to be bound or limited, I had to do the difficult thing. I had to let the scar tissue be broken up.

Likewise, I knew I couldn't surrender in this new fight. I'd already experienced the alternative. Remember, fear had already been my master and had stolen so much from me. I decided that no matter how long this "spiritual therapy" was going to take, I would not surrender and let the enemy put another scar on my heart. I was determined to not let him win because I didn't want to be put back into bondage! I knew I would have to continue to resist him (James 4:7).

So, I picked up my sword and shield and set my heart like a flint. At the same time, I was going through physical therapy and seeing very *slow* progress with my shoulder, so I just assumed that this fight would take a long time. It was not unusual for me to go to therapy on Monday and see a quarter of an inch improvement, only to go back on Friday and see that I not only lost that minuscule gain but lost another quarter inch as well.

I really wasn't looking forward to the fight. At first, just being in it seemed like failure. Like I said before, the enemy was trying to convince me that I hadn't changed and that God really hadn't done such a great work in me. It can be tempting to think we have failed *just* because we are struggling, but the truth is, *being in the battle* is not failure! It's what you do *in* the battle that determines if you fail. We only lose when we stop fighting and get into agreement with him. Satan's not going to stop trying, and while he can be persistent, he doesn't have the fruit of the spirit, but we do!

To my surprise, before I even realized what was happening, the battle was over! It ended up not being a painful and arduous "spiritual therapy." Actually, I didn't even notice it at first. I had mentally prepared myself for a long and painful battle with fear, but the next thing I knew, fear's voice sounded so far away. It was more like an occasional *whisper*. His threats seemed powerless. What I didn't realize at first was that I had *already* been going through "spiritual therapy." Even in my weakened state, I had been holding onto God's promises. Even though I was struggling with doubt, my seemingly inefficient stand against the enemy was enough to prevent him from binding me with a sling in an attempt to chisel his lies onto my soul. The "win" might not have been pretty or even effortless, but a win is a win! Despite how close he had felt, the devil had been unsuccessful in his attempt to form a negative soul belief.

So, knowing *about* soul beliefs doesn't keep the enemy from trying to cause more of them. However, knowing **how** he tries to form them allows us to protect ourselves when we are hurt and vulnerable.

10

GOD DOESN'T WASTE ANYTHING

LET THE FATHER REWRITE YOUR STORY

I'm a formula person. I wish I had the perfect five-step regiment or precise blueprint for uncovering and getting free from these negative soul beliefs, but I don't believe there is just *one way*. Our God is way more capable, creative, and personal than that!

Your life and your relationship with God are unique. However, I do believe there is a necessary starting place, and again, it doesn't begin with you working to change yourself! Instead, it is about being transparent and vulnerable and allowing the Lord of Glory, the perfect Father, to minister to you. Believe me when I tell you, His work is beautiful and gentle. While we might be able to modify our outward behavior to some degree, the Holy Spirit is the One who heals and changes our souls.

When I was in a season in which I struggled with works, telling me to study God's word and pray more would **not** have been helpful because that's just where I was. I had done that for years. This required something different. I needed to go deeper, past the religious jargon in my own head, so that God's Word could genuinely *pierce* my wounded soul. It's almost as if the scars were too thick for the truth to penetrate the deepest parts of me. The written Word was in my *head*, but I needed the *other* Word, Jesus Himself, to heal the scars so His truths could seep through and take residence in the recesses of my heart.

So when my "showdown" began, I had no plan per se. I would just go down for another round of wrestling, trying to wrangle the truth out of God. After a few days of trying to read the Word and complaining, I mean praying, God showed up. As I said before, the "meetings" quickly morphed into worship. I would just sit or lay in His presence with worship music in the background and that's when I finally met my Papa!

Before I even knew what was happening, I didn't care about all the questions with which I had started. I began to encounter the Beautiful Father. His presence, His glory, His kindness, and His love began to change me.

As He began to dismantle the elaborate foundation that *I* had created, religious beliefs started flying out the window. Condemnation was defeated. Works were crushed! No longer did I feel the pressure or requirement to read the Word or pray; now, *I wanted to*!

I had discovered the goodness of the Father and that was enough for me. The truth is, He swept me off my feet. I had always loved Jesus, but for the first time, I began to receive the love of the Father!

"Did something great happen every time?" Nope! There were days that I didn't "feel" Him, but I kept coming back. I wasn't religious about it though. If I missed a day, I didn't beat myself up. However, I quickly found that I couldn't wait to meet again. Once I truly encountered His love, I was hooked. I became addicted to His presence, and the religious "requirements" were of no interest. I just wanted HIM!

So I would say the most essential ingredient on your part is a willingness to lay it all down. Those of us who are strong and deal with legalism can sometimes be dogmatic. If fear is mixed in, you have a real problem because you're afraid to be deceived, so you dig in your heels even further. I believe the Bible is the final say on all matters, so *nothing* you feel that God is showing you will *ever* be contrary to the Word. It may, however, be contrary to your long-held, conscious beliefs! However, those are precisely the beliefs we want God to go after, right?

My simple recommendation is that you get alone and put on your favorite worship music. You may have heard of soaking prayer/worship. If not, it's simply getting alone with God and "soaking" in His presence. Have you ever wanted to reuse a jar that had a label on it? We reuse jars quite often in our home. In order to get the labels off the jars, we soak the jar in water until the label peels right off. I like to think of soaking with the Lord like that. The jar doesn't have to **do** anything while it's soaking; it just sits in the water, *letting the water do the work* to loosen the *old label*. So what I'm recommending is that you just sit in his *label-removing water*.

Don't worry about praying at first. Just invite His presence and ask Him to speak to you. Just rest! I know that can be a challenge. It can be hard to shut off all the thoughts swirling in your mind. As you think about Him and all He has done, don't be surprised if you see or hear something that might sound strange. Remember, I saw the movie <u>Annie</u> in my mind's eye when God wanted to talk to me about living like an orphan. You might hear a word or a saying. Don't brush it off as *your* thoughts. If something comes up that stands out to you or seems out of left field, ask the Holy Spirit if He is trying to show you something. Remember, God is in you, so when He speaks, He can sound like your thoughts. The more you do this, the more you get to know Him, and the more you will be able to discern His voice from yours. Don't be afraid to be honest with Him. He knows your every thought and STILL loves you!

God can reveal a negative soul belief to you while you're going about your everyday life as well. Once you are aware they exist, God might show you during a "disagreement" with your spouse that you have a negative soul belief about them, yourself, or marriage. As these soul beliefs are brought to the surface, all we need to do is take them to the Father and be honest with Him. He is the One who heals the wounds that created these negative soul beliefs in the first place. He lovingly molds, stretches and, remodels the scars, so He can create new, positive soul beliefs. In addition to this, when those areas are healed, and the truth is believed *by your soul*, quoting the scriptures takes on an entirely new meaning! This is when we see the power of the Word in action. It is when the lies are dealt with, rather than ignored, that we can stand on the truth of God's Word like never before.

The Journey

Jesus refers to us as His bride, and if you are married, you've already realized that you can't get to know your spouse overnight. So this entire book is not about you finding "The Right Formula" that fixes all your issues. Instead, it is about removing the barriers that are preventing you from an intimate relationship with the Beloved Father, Son, and Holy Spirit.

We are marvelous masterpieces, works of art in *progress*. However, He doesn't wait to love us until we are "completed." He sees us as completed. His love for us cannot be deterred by what we do or don't do. Thankfully, when we recognize just how good He really is, and we begin to expose the lies, we enter a deeper relationship with the Lover of our soul!

Just as a husband and wife are supposed to spend their lifetimes getting to know one another, we are doing the same with our Savior. This is a journey, but I don't want that word to sound scary to you. This is not the kind of trip that is long and arduous. Yes indeed, you may have lots of painful wounds tucked away, but that doesn't mean that this is going to be excruciating and long. However, I won't lie to you either and tell you that it is pain free. The good news is, once you *really* encounter His Love, the rest of the adventure gets easier. When these barriers are removed, you can sense His presence, which makes the journey worth it all.

We are all walking through the same broken world. While all our journeys are unique, pain and disappointment visit all of us. However, we have a Savior who loves us immeasurably and can heal even the deepest of wounds.

Whether you were abandoned, used, abused, or all the above, I am so sorry that you went through that! God never wanted or caused those things to happen to you. He is for you and not against you. He wants to be your friend and help you through it. He wants to hold you and heal you. He is a good Father.

I'm here to tell you that this is not the end of your story! I'm convinced that when we truly know that God loves us, it changes everything. Despite all that has happened, He has really good plans for you! He wants you to know that He knows how to take all that has happened and make something beautiful out of it.

The popular Christian music artist, MercyMe, has a song called "Dear Younger Me."[1] Just as you might imagine, it's asking what you would say to the younger version of yourself. My favorite part is when it says we are not meant to carry around the heavy burdens of our old life. The cross is meant to be the end of all that.

Think about this truth… you were never meant to carry "**all that**" beyond the cross. Whatever "all that" is for you personally, whatever you personally can put in those quotation marks, you were never meant to carry it beyond the cross. However, sadly, many of us do. We haul it around for years!

That's why I think it is so crucial that we are able to be authentic with ourselves and with God. I'm not sure if it's because we assume it's improper or because we are afraid, but many of us don't think we can be completely honest with God. **Spoiler alert**: He already knows what you're thinking and believing anyway, and He still loves you!

You were designed to have an awesome relationship with God! He is crazy about you! You were not created to merely become a Christian and then live a "religious" life! Jesus, Holy Spirit, and the Father want a *relationship* with you! Remember when I said earlier that He doesn't take us from our B.C. (Before Christ) life-of-bondage, simply to put us back in religious chains? It's the truth! He doesn't want you to be enslaved to works, condemnation, performance, shame, or anything else. He wants an intimate relationship!

You see, the Creator of all things is the same doting Father that stands before you now, asking you to give it all to Him. Doting means: extremely and uncritically fond of someone; adoring.[2] He wants you to be free. He wants you to be able to receive His love. He thinks about you ALL the time! (Psalm 40:17).

His Story

I may not know your individual story, but I can confidently tell you that God's heart is for you. His heart is broken over the terrible things you've experienced. However, His plan to give you an abundant life has not changed!

The fascinating thing about God is that He doesn't waste anything. If you hand Him your pain, He will bring beauty out of it. It's another of His specialties. He is a God that restores! He knows how to take what was intended for evil and turn it into strength and beauty. He turns our ashes into beauty and our mourning into joy.

When I read Isaiah 61, my heart melts. This is the heart of the *Father*, delivered through Jesus. Please pay close attention to the areas that I have bolded.

> The SPIRIT of the Lord God is upon me, because the Lord has anointed and qualified me to preach the Gospel of good tidings to the meek, the **poor**, and **afflicted**; He has sent me to **bind up and heal the brokenhearted**, to proclaim **liberty to the (physical and spiritual) captives** and the **opening of the prison and of the eyes to those who are bound**,
>
> —Isaiah 61:1, AMPC

So let's look at a couple of those words. The word "bind" has several meanings. One definition is "to wrap tightly."[3] Let's take the example of a broken bone. For more damage not to occur, the broken bone needs to be stabilized and kept safe by wrapping it tightly or putting it in a cast. This is necessary for healing to take place. Notice that Jesus didn't just say bind, but He added the word "heal" because He is the Great Physician. He knows better than anyone else what our hearts need, so He not only bandages our broken hearts, He heals them!

Another meaning of the word "bind" is "to combine with (a substance) through chemical bonding.[4] I think that's so cool! His love is the binding substance that causes a chemical bonding and puts our hearts back together. His love is the ingredient that heals us.

Another important word in that same verse is "proclaim." Jesus came to proclaim liberty to both the physical and spiritual captives. The word *proclaim* means more than just "to say." According to Dictionary.com it means to announce or declare in an **official** or formal manner. Jesus doesn't just *say* we are free, He has the official or **legal right** to make it so. He has the authority to set us free, and He came to do just that. Notice, too, that He included both the physical and spiritual captives.

Verse 2 of Isaiah 61 says:

> To proclaim the acceptable year of the Lord (the year of His favor) and the day of vengeance of our God, **to comfort all who mourn**. (AMPC)

Most of us relate the word "mourn" with the loss of a loved one. And while that is often the case, the word mourn can also mean to feel regret or sadness about the loss or disappearance of something. The Father sent Jesus to comfort ALL who mourn! It doesn't matter what it is that you are mourning. It may be the loss of a marriage, a broken dream, a shattered promise, a crushed hope, or the loss of a loved one. He came to comfort you. He wants to be right there, in your face, comforting you! He wants you to know how very close He is to you.

Then, we get to verse 3. He doesn't want us to just be comforted, He wants us to have joy! Check this out:

> To grant (**consolation and joy**) **to those who mourn** in Zion-**to give them an ornament (a garland or diadem) of beauty instead of ashes**, the **oil of joy instead of mourning**, the **garment (expressive) of praise instead of a heavy burdened and failing spirit**- that they may be called oaks of righteousness (lofty,

strong, and magnificent, distinguished for uprightness, justice, and right standing with God), the planting of the Lord, that He may be glorified. (AMPC)

Look at that! He not only provides consolation, but He gives us JOY. Our Father goes over and above. He's not satisfied with *just* healing us and consoling us, but He wants to move us into joy!

And if all of that wasn't enough, He goes even further. He says that we can *exchange* our ashes—which represents mourning, repentance, grief, humility, brokenness, and more—for a beautiful, royal diadem! Why is that so important? Well, according to Wikipedia, the word diadem is a type of crown, specifically an ornamental headband worn by monarchs and others as a *badge* of royalty. The term originally referred to the embroidered white silk ribbon, ending in a knot and two fringed strips often draped over the shoulders, that surrounded the head of the **king** to denote his authority.[5]

What a beautiful picture! We hand Him the useless, burned up leftovers or ashes and He gives us the valuable crown of royalty. That crown gives us the authority to move out from beneath the old life, bound and controlled by fear, destruction, and pain. Who does that? *Who trades something so incredibly valuable, only to get disgusting ashes in return?* OUR FATHER! He is that mind-boggling good!

Now, let's jump down a little further in chapter 61 of Isaiah:

> **Instead of your (former) shame you shall have a twofold recompense; instead of dishonor and reproach (your people) shall rejoice in their portion.** Therefore, in their land they shall possess double (what they had forfeited); everlasting joy shall be theirs. For I the Lord love justice; I hate robbery and wrong with

violence or a burnt offering. And **I will faithfully give them their recompense in truth**, and I will make an everlasting covenant or league with them. And their offspring shall be known among the nations and their descendants among their peoples. All who see them (in their prosperity) will **recognize and acknowledge that they are the people who the Lord has blessed**

—Isaiah 61:7-9, AMPC

Our God is the initiator of restoration. In the above verse, He says, **"Instead of your (former) shame you shall have a twofold recompense..."** Recompense means to make amends to someone for loss or harm suffered; compensate.[6] If you are hit and injured by another driver, who is at fault, it is their insurance company who is going to pay you for the repairs and injuries. Now, was it the other driver's insurance company that hit you? No, they did not cause your suffering. However, they will be the one providing compensation. In the same way, your loving Father was not the one that caused your hurt, rejection or pain. However, He offers to give you recompense. As a matter of fact, He promises to!

In addition, we can see from this verse that He also takes our dishonor, shame, and disgrace. That means even if it was by our own choices and no one else's fault, for what we are ashamed of, He will take it. So it doesn't matter if the shame is from what someone did to us or what we have done ourselves; God will receive it! He's not afraid of it. He's not disgusted by it.

There are so many beautiful promises in Isaiah 61 and 62. I would encourage you to read them all since I'm only highlighting a few. Here are a just a few more of His beautiful promises from Isaiah 62:2-7:

- He ascribes HIS righteousness to you.
- You shall be called by a new name which the mouth of the Lord shall name.
- You shall also be so beautiful and prosperous as to be thought of as a **crown of glory and honor in the hand of your God.**
- **You shall no more be termed Forsaken,** nor shall your land be called Desolate any more.
- You shall be called Hephzibah **(My delight is in her),** and your land be called Beulah **(married); for the Lord delights in you, and your land shall be married (owned and protected by the Lord).** For as a young man marries a virgin (O Jerusalem), so shall your sons marry you; and **as the bridegroom rejoices over the bride, so shall your God rejoice over you.** (AMPC)

You and I are crowns of glory in the hand of our God! We are His **reward**—even if you don't think you're a reward, you are! He thinks that you and I are worth the sacrifice He made. He is not afraid of our junk! We can give it to Him. We don't have to try to hide it because He truly delights in us. He is where our help comes from. Though we were once forsaken, He has now taken us in. We are His bride, and He rejoices over us!

We were not designed to limp through life. The words you read above in Isaiah are intimate words because He is an **intimate** God. Your Father can take all the horrible things you've walked through and turn them around for your good because He is the Master Restorer. He did not orchestrate the pain in your life because He is a good Father! The enemy wanted to crush and defeat you, but God can work all things out for the good of those who love Him, who have been called according to His purpose (Romans 8:28). That means you! You've been called according to HIS purpose.

I can honestly say that while I wish things had been different in my childhood, I have embraced them. My story is beautiful to God. **Your story** is beautiful to God! I want you to REFUSE to accept that your history is your destiny. It doesn't have to be! He is crazy about you and wants you to live like you are loved because YOU ARE! In the hands of your perfect Father, your story can intersect with His and become the ultimate love story!

I love the words of the song, "Out of Hiding" by Steffany Gretzinger.[7] It beautifully conveys the truth that everything that hindered God's love in our life will be used by God to become part of our redemption story. I don't believe God is looking for "scarless" hearts. I also don't believe God erases the scars on our hearts. Instead, I believe He rewrites beautiful new messages on them. With His own, once wounded, beautiful hand, He creates a beautiful mosaic, an epic masterpiece!

MY PRAYER FOR YOU

Papa,

It is Your anointing that breaks the yoke of bondage! I thank You for revealing Your abundant love to each person reading this book. I declare over them that they are free! Holy Spirit, thank You for showing them what the Father thinks about and feels toward them. Reveal Your heart to them! Open their eyes to the truth so they can walk intimately with You. Thank You for healing their wounds and strengthening them with Your love and might. I pray they will walk in the knowledge of their adoption, fully understanding who they are, refusing to live according to their original birth certificate.

Thank You, Holy Spirit, for identifying the negative soul beliefs that are hindering their relationship with You. Heal the wounds ,and rewrite the messages into Your glorious truths.

I pray that an encounter with You will crush every misconception, stronghold, and lie. I know Your love for them is beyond words and that You find pleasure in them, so I ask You to reveal that to them in such a measure that they will never be the same. May they know beyond any shadow of a doubt how much You love them! Thank You for setting them free from all forms of bondage.

May they experience You as their Lover, the Rescuer for whom their hearts have always longed.

"Beloved, I wish above all things that thou mayest prosper and be in health, even as thy soul prospereth."
(3 John 1:2, KJV)

GOD'S GOODNESS SCRIPTURES:

Psalm 107:1 (TPT)

Let everyone give all their praise and thanks to the Lord! Here's why – he's better than anyone could ever imagine. Yes, he's always loving and kind, and his faithful love never ends.

Psalm 145:9 (TPT)

God, everyone sees your goodness, for your tender love is blended into everything you do.

John 10:10 (TPT) (emphasis added)

A thief has only one thing in mind – he wants to steal, slaughter, and destroy. **But I have come to give you everything in abundance, more than you expect – life in its fullness until you overflow!**

Psalm 34:8 (TPT)

Drink deeply of the pleasures of this God. Experience for yourself the joyous mercies he gives to all who turn to hid themselves in him.

Psalm 85:2 (TPT)

You've forgiven our many sins and covered every one of them in your love.

Psalm 84:11 (TPT)

For the Lord God is brighter than the brilliance of a sunrise! Wrapping himself around me like a shield, he is so generous with his gifts of grace and glory. Those who walk along his paths with integrity will never lack one thing they need, for he provides it all!

Psalm 31:19

Lord, how wonderful you are! You have stored up so many good things for us, like a treasure chest heaped up and spilling over with blessings – all for those who honor and worship you! Everybody knows what you can do for those who turn and hide themselves in you.

Jeremiah 29:11 (AMP)

For I know the thoughts and plans that I have for you, says the Lord, thoughts and plans for welfare and peace and not for evil, to give you hope in your final outcome.

Luke 18:19 (TPT)

Jesus answered, "Why would you call me wonderful when there is only one who is wonderful – and that is God alone?

1 John 4:16 (TPT)

We have come into an intimate experience with God's love, and we trust in the love he has for us. God is love! Those who are living in love are living in God, and God lives through them.

YOUR RIGHTEOUSNESS SCRIPTURES:

Romans 3:21-24 (TPT) (emphasis added)

But now, independently of the law, the righteousness of God is tangible and brought to light through Jesus, the Anointed One. This is the righteousness that the Scriptures prophesied would come. It is God's righteousness made visible through the faithfulness of Jesus Christ. **And now all who believe in Him receive that gift.** For there is really no difference between us, for we all have sinned and are in need of the glory of God. Yet through **His powerful declaration of acquittal, God freely gives away His righteousness. His gift of love and favor now cascades over us, all because Jesus, the Anointed One, has liberated us from the guilt, punishment, and power of sin!**

Philippians 3:9 (AMP)

And that I may (actually) be found and known as in Him, not having any (self-achieved) righteousness that can be called my own, based on my obedience to the Law's demands (ritualistic uprightness and supposed right standing with God thus acquired), but possessing that (genuine righteousness) which comes through faith in Christ (the Anointed One), the (truly) right standing with God, which comes from God by (saving) faith.

Galatians 2:16 (AMP)

Yet we know that a man is justified or reckoned righteous and in right standing with God not by works of the Law but (only) through faith and (absolute) reliance on and adherence to and trust in Jesus Christ (the Messiah, the Anointed One). (Therefore) even we (ourselves) have believed on Christ Jesus, in order to be justified by faith in Christ and not by works of the Law (for we cannot be justified by any observance of the ritual of the Law given by Moses), because by keeping legal rituals and by works no human being can ever be justified (declared righteous and put in right standing with God).

1 Peter 2:24 (AMP)

He personally bore our sins in His (own) body on the tree (as on an altar and offered Himself on it), that we might die (cease to exist) to sin and live to righteousness. By His wounds you have been healed.

Romans 3:22-24 (AMP)

Namely, the righteousness of God which comes by believing with personal trust and confident reliance on Jesus Christ (the Messiah). (And it is mean) for all who believe. For there is no distinction since all have sinned and are falling short of the honor and glory which God bestows and receives. (All) are justified and made upright and in right standing with God, freely and gratuitously by His grace (His unmerited favor and mercy), through the redemption which is (provided) in Christ Jesus.

Romans 4:4-5 (AMP)

Now to a laborer, his wages are not counted as a favor or a gift, but as an obligation (something owed to him). But to one who, not working (by the Law), trusts (believes fully) in Him Who justifies the ungodly, his faith is credited to him as righteousness (the standing acceptable to God).

Galatians 2:20-21 (AMP)

I have been crucified with Christ (in Him I have shared His crucifixion); it is no longer I who live, but Christ (the Messiah) lives in me; and the life I now live in the body I live by faith in (by adherence to and reliance on and complete trust in) the Son of God, Who loved me and gave Himself up for me. (Therefore, I do not treat God's gracious gift as something of minor importance and defeat its very purpose); I do not set aside and invalidate and frustrate and nullify the grace (unmerited favor) of God. For if justification (righteousness, acquittal from guilt) comes through (observing the ritual of) the Law, then Christ (the Messiah) died groundlessly and to no purpose and in vain. (His death was then wholly superfluous.)

Romans 5:17 (AMP)

For if because of one man's trespass (lapse, offense) death reigned through that one, much more surely will those who receive (God's) overflowing grace (unmerited favor) and the free gift of righteousness (putting them into right standing with Himself) reign as kings in life through the one Man Jesus Christ (the Messiah, the Anointed One.)

Romans 8:1-4 (AMP)

Therefore, (there is) now no condemnation (no adjudging guilty of wrong) for those who are in Christ Jesus, who live (and) walk not after the dictates of the flesh, but after the dictates of the Spirit. (John 3:18) For the law of the Spirit of life (which is) in Christ Jesus (the law of our new being) has freed me from the law of sin and death. For God has done what the Law could not do, (its power) being weakened by the flesh (the entire nature of man without the Holy Spirit). Sending His own Son in the guise of sinful flesh and as an offering for sin, (God) condemned sin in the flesh (subdued, overcame, deprived it of its power over all who accept that sacrifice), (Lev. 7:37) So that the righteous and just requirement of the Law might be fully met in us who live and move not in the ways of flesh but in the ways of the Spirit (our lives governed not by the standards and according to the dictates of the flesh, but controlled by the Holy Spirit).

Romans 10:4-5 (AMP)

For Christ is the end of the Law (the limit at which it ceases to be, for the Law leads up to Him Who is the fulfillment of its types, and in Him the purpose which it was designed to accomplish is fulfilled. That is, the purpose of the Law is fulfilled in Him) as the means of righteousness (right relationship to God) for everyone who trusts in and adheres to and relies on Him. For Moses writes that the man who (can) practice the righteousness (perfect conformity to God's will) which is based on the Law (with all its intricate demands) shall live by it. (Lev. 18:5)

YOUR ADOPTION SCRIPTURES:

Galatians 4:5 (TPT) Yet all of this was so that he would redeem and set free all those held hostage to the written law so that we would receive our freedom and a full legal adoption as his children.

Romans 8:15 (TPT) And you did not receive the "spirit of religious duty," leading you back into the fear of never being good enough. But you have received the "Spirit of Full Acceptance," enfolding you into the family of God. And you will never feel orphaned, for as he rises up within us, our spirts join him in saying the words of tender affection, "Beloved Father!" For the Holy Spirit makes God's fatherhood real to us as he whispers into our innermost being, "You are God's beloved child!" And since we are his true children, we qualify to share all his treasures, for indeed, we are heirs of God himself. And since we are joined to Christ, we also inherit all that he is and all that he has. We will experience being co-glorified with him provided that we accept his sufferings as our own.

Ephesians 1:5 (TPT) For it was always in his perfect plan to adopt us as his delightful children, through our union with

Jesus, the Anointed One, so that his tremendous love that cascades over us would glorify his grace-for the same love he has for his Beloved One, Jesus, he has for us. And this unfolding plan brings him great pleasure!

NOTES

2. When Everything Changed

1. Duke, Roby. "Carpenter (Do What You Got to Do)" on *Not The Same*, 1982, Vivid Sound, cassette.

3. Facing The Past

1. Big Daddy Weave, "Redeemed," 2012 on *Love Come to Life*, Curb Records, Fervent Records, Compact-Disc.

4. The Showdown

1. 2020 showdown. In: **Lexico**.com, Available at: https://www.**lexico**.com/**definition**/showdown [Accessed 03/07/2020].

5. I Don't Trust You?

1. 2020 cornerstone. In: vocabulary.com, Available at: https://www.vocabulary.com/dictionary/cornerstone [Accessed 03/07/2020].
2. Merriam-Webster's Collegiate Dictionary (10th ed.). (1999). Merriam-Webster Incorporated.

6. I Have To Be Good Enough?

1. Augustine, of Hippo, Saint, 354-430. The Confessions of St. Augustine : Books I-IX (Selections). New York :Prentice-Hall, 19421931.

7. There Is Something Wrong With Me

1. 2020 shame. In: vocabulary.com, Available at: https://www.vocabulary.com/dictionary/shame [Accessed 03/07/2020].
2. Merriam-Webster's Collegiate Dictionary (10th ed.). (1999). Merriam-Webster Incorporated.

8. The Beautiful Journey

1. Frost, Jack. *Experiencing Father's Embrace*. Destiny Image Publishers, 2006.
2. adopt.org
3. Ibid.
4. W. M. Ramsay, *A Historical Commentary on St. Paul's Epistle to the Galatians*, Baker Book House, Grand Rapids, MI.
5. Ibid.
6. Ibid.

9. Scar Tissue

1. Quinn, E. (2019, June 24). *Adhesion Medical Causes and Types*. Verywellhealth.Com. https://www.verywellfit.com/what-is-an-adhesion-3120337
2. Ibid.
3. Ibid.
4. Clear Passage Physical Therapy. (n.d.). *Treating Adhesions and Scar Tissue*. Clearpassage.Com. http://www.clearpassage.com/adhesions-and-scar-tissue/
5. Ibid.

10. God Doesn't Waste Anything

1. Mercy Me, "Dear Younger Me," May 16, 2016, *Welcome to the New*, Columbia Records, 2014.
2. "Oxford Languages and Google - English." *Oxford Languages*, languages.oup.com/google-dictionary-en/.
3. Ibid.
4. Ibid.
5. *diadem*. (2020). Wikipedia. https://en.wikipedia.org/wiki/Diadem
6. "Oxford Languages and Google - English." *Oxford Languages*, languages.oup.com/google-dictionary-en/.
7. Steffany Gretzinger. "Out of Hiding," *The Undoing*. Bethel Music, 2014.

ACKNOWLEDGMENTS

Jesus & Holy Spirit, I will never be able to thank You enough for introducing me to the Father! I love You. Thank You for loving me!

Roger, I'm so proud to call you my husband. Thank you for your steadfast love and commitment to our family. Life has been an adventure, and I'm so grateful that you've been by my side. You are the fulfillment of God's promises to me. Thank you for supporting my dreams. I love you!

Hope, Isaac, Luke & Ethan, how could I ever express the joy I've experienced being your mom? Beautiful Hope, your arrival truly brought "hope" back into our lives. You are an incredible daughter and treasured friend. You hold a special place in my heart. Creative Isaac, your arrival brought laughter back into our lives. You are uniquely designed by the Father for great things. You hold a special place in my heart. Courageous Luke, your arrival brought healing into our lives. You are an answer to prayer and so worth the wait. You hold a special place in my heart. Compassionate Ethan, you are the whipped topping to our family. Your love and kindness are evident to everyone. You hold a special place in my heart. I love each of you more than you'll ever know. God blessed me beyond my wildest dreams by giving me my heart's desires through each of you!

Jeff and Jenny, thank you for your unconditional love for my family and me. Your encouragement has meant the world to us. God used both of you to help me to pick up His gifts again. I will forever be grateful for your friendship.

Thank you to the following amazing women that prayed and prophesied to me through this journey. Candace, Cherlyn, Jackie, Jenny, Lora, Michelle, Nicole, and Rachel. You ladies are incredible, and I am so honored to know you.

Thank you to everyone at Messenger Books who gave me so much support and encouragement. Each of you played such an important role in helping me get this book across the finish line. Special thanks to Jeremiah, Teresa, and Krissy. I'm honored to work with such incredible people. And, to Kevin, my amazing editor, your belief and support of this book means more to me than you know. Thank you to each of you from the bottom of my heart.

ABOUT THE AUTHOR

Tammy Hernandez is a wife, mom, speaker, mentor, teacher, and self-proclaimed recovering legalist. After spending too many years trying to earn God's love, she finally fell into the unconditional, loving arms of her Heavenly Father.

Serving as marriage mentors at New Life Church in Colorado Springs, she and her husband of more than twenty-seven years, have walked with couples through both nuptial bliss and marital crisis. Their brutally honest and vulnerable approach is shared, not only with those they've mentored, but also with those that attend the small group classes they offer.

Tammy is currently sharing her insights, victories, and struggles with fellow believers at prophetic conferences, women's gatherings, youth conferences, and more. Driven no longer by performance, she is having a blast watching God reveal His unadulterated love to others through teaching and prophetic ministry. In every area that she serves, it is her heart's desire to see others experience the healing touch of the Savior, not only in their marriages, but in every area of their lives. She has the privilege of being a wife to Roger and mom to her four amazing children. They make their home in beautiful Colorado.